When Wee Wullie was sitting up and beginning to look like a human being, the minister suddenly announced he would like to look in on the invalid.

'Hold on!' I cried in alarm. 'Wait till I warn him.'

I went coughing away to break the news to Wee Wullie. 'The minister wants to come and see you.'

'O God!' exclaimed Wee Wullie and disappeared beneath the bedclothes.

Nothing would induce him to show his face. I heard H.J. coming and going without a word spoken. Then – there was more to the minister than met the eye – I heard a surprising sound. Music! H.J. had gone back to his study and picked up his fiddle. Now he was marching along the passage, into the kitchen, into the wee bedroom, playing a lively Scots reel. I followed behind to see what would happen. Presently a nose appeared above the covers. The next thing I saw was the minister perched on the bed, fiddling away for dear life with Wee Wullie sitting up and jiggling in time to the tune.

Also in Arrow by Lavinia Derwent

A Breath of Border Air
God Bless the Borders!

LAVINIA DERWENT

Lady of the Manse

Illustrations by Elizabeth Haines

ARROW BOOKS

To H.J.
In memory

Arrow Books Limited
17-21 Conway Street, London W1P 6JD

An imprint of the Hutchinson Publishing Group

London Melbourne Sydney Auckland
Johannesburg and agencies throughout
the world

First published by Hutchinson 1983
Arrow edition 1985

Printed and bound in Great Britain by
Anchor Brendon Limited, Tiptree, Essex

ISBN 0 09 939620 3

1. In Between

The hub of my universe was the farmhouse kitchen. It was the heart of the house, especially if Jessie was there bustling about her business. When I turn my thoughts back, this is where the clock begins to tick, in the stone-flagged kitchen with all its homely smells and sounds.

As a child I sat on the rug beside cats and collies watching Jessie baking, churning, ironing, making jam, listening to her tart tongue as she scolded the servant-lass and dodging out of her way when she came to dump another pot on the fire. Hers were the first words I remember hearing. They have seeped into my brain and I remember them to this day.

Jessie was the shepherd's sister and lived in one of the nearby cottages – the herd's hoose – but came in every day to rule the kitchen in the big hoose. She was more than a servant to me. She was my best friend, my mentor, my comforter, the most important person in my young life.

It was to her roughened hand I clung when taking my first steps, to her I turned for solace. My parents were preoccupied with my elder brother and sister, and later with smaller fry who claimed their attention. So I was only an in-between, nobody special in the family, except to Jessie who sometimes took notice of me, even if it was only to say, 'Get oot ma road!'

True, her tongue was sharp enough to clip cloots. To cut cloth. I bore the brunt of it many a time, deadlier than a blow; yet inside that crusty shell was a soft centre that was worth reaching. If I coaxed her she would tell me fascinating stories, all about 'beasties', which fired my imagination so much that I determined to invent characters for myself and make storytelling my career.

But the best character was Jessie herself and I did not need to invent her.

The farmhouse was hidden away in the Border hills a mile from the main road, reached only by a bumpy track. So there was no passing traffic, no strangers to come to our door, only tramps begging for a night's shelter. And as I had so few outsiders to talk to, it was to Jessie I turned when I wanted to unburden myself. Even when I was leaving childhood behind.

Now here I was with the biggest problem of my life turning to her once again for advice.

And as always it was Jessie who put everything in a nutshell. 'The back's aye made for the burden.' One of her trite but true sayings which has stood me in good stead throughout the years.

'But Jessie . . .'

'Nane o' your buts, lassie. Ye're no' gaun awa' to the ends o' the earth.'

This from Jessie who had never ventured out of sight of the Cheviot hills! And who did not believe in the existence of places she had not seen with her own eyes. Newcastle lay beyond the Carter Bar. (So they said!) Edinburgh was some sixty miles in the opposite direction. (Maybe!) It was all hearsay. How could she be certain they were *there*?

But she knew all about commonsense. Rummlegumption, she called it; and if I had any it was thanks to her thumping it into me, often painfully. Jessie saw everything in black and white. Right was right: wrong was wrong. No in-betweens.

I was an in-between myself now, neither a bairn nor a grown-up. I had never heard the word teenager, but that's what I was, I suppose. A teenager about to leave the nest.

'Will you miss me, Jessie?' I asked her one of my foolish questions.

'Ay, like a sair thoomb.'

There was no doubt I would miss her. 'But I'll come back often to see you,' I promised.

'Uh-huh!' She gave me a look which could have meant anything, then spoke of practical things. 'See here! This is what ye do.'

She was showing me how to make a clootie dumpling. A confusing operation since Jessie never worked from a recipe but cooked by instinct, not bothering about exact quantities. A handful of flour, a wee drop of this and that. 'A nieve-fou o' floor, a wee tait o' sugar, a wee dad o' butter . . .' It was too difficult to follow, so I just stood and watched, letting Jessie do all the work.

When the dumpling was bubbling in the pot I ran outside and climbed on to the garden dyke. Jock-the-herd was mending the gate which had come off its hinges. I often got blamed for swinging on it but today there was a different culprit. Grumphy the pig.

'That danged soo!' grunted the shepherd, not usually given to strong language. 'She's gettin' her throat cut next week, an' serve her richt!'

I gave a shiver of sympathy for Grumphy though I knew the inevitable fate of all farm animals. The slaughter of the soo would mean hams hanging from the kitchen ceiling, tasty meals of spareribs, faggots, pigs' puddings, potted head; and think how often I had enjoyed playing with the bladder (the blether) when Jock blew it up into an opaque football. But I never could stomach hearing the terrified squeals as the shepherd sharpened his knives, and ran like the wind out of earshot till the dread deed was done.

Next week! I would be well out of earshot by then.

I gave a shiver for my own sake, not for Grumphy's, and asked the same silly question I had put to Jessie. I needed some assurance.

'Will you miss me, Jock?'

'Toots!' said the herd.

Did that mean yes or no? He was uncommunicative at the best of times. Now, with his mouth full of nails, I was lucky to get an answer at all. But it seemed he had more to say, for he spat the nails iinto his roughened hand. 'Man-lassie, ye'll still be in the Borders.'

'Yes, but it's a different kind of Borders. Berwick-shire.'

'Ay,' agreed the herd. 'I dinna ken muckle aboot Berwickshire, bar the sheep. There's some guid grazin' doon there.'

'But it's not a farm I'm going to, Jock. It's a Manse.'

'Dod! So it is! A'weel, ye'd better get doon aff that dyke an' be a bit mair perjink.'

I slid off the dyke and straightened my skirt. Being perjink meant being precise, particular, neat, finicky, minding one's p's and q's. All the things I wasn't. That was what worried me about the new life that awaited me. Being perjink.

'It'll be a terrible strain,' I sighed. A teenager with all the cares of the world on her shoulders.

'Toots!' said Jock, whatever that meant.

All very well for him. He could still stay in his familiar surroundings, mend dykes, calve cows, kill Grumphy, help with the harvest, and tramp around the hills with Jed and Jess at his heels. *He* would remain in Roxburghshire within sight of the Cheviots and the Carter Bar, while I was going 'down country' into an alien land filled with strangers. My back would never carry the burden.

I had felt faintly flattered at first. Now I was terrified. Normally, my lordly brother, the eldest in the family, almost ten years my senior, took no notice of me at all. I did not expect it. Who was I compared to him and his learning? Hebrew no less! And goodness knows what else he had been taught at the university and the divinity college in Edinburgh. Enough to get letters after his name. Not just an MA with honours. BD as well. Bachelor of Divinity.

Now he was a fully fledged minister of the kirk and had served his apprenticeship in a great city church in Edinburgh.

The next step up the ladder was to 'preach for a place' so that he could have a church of his own. This he had successfully done, and now he had been called to a parish in Berwickshire.

I used to wonder about these calls. Folk talked about preachers having 'heard the call' to join the ministry. From above, I presumed. 'Was't no' another soond ye heard?' a doubting elder once asked a young minister after hearing his halting sermon. But my brother had been dedicated to the church almost since the cradle, aided and abetted by Mother, so *he* seemed genuinely to have heard the right sound.

Though he seemed set and staid to me, he was not a holier-than-thou type. I suppose in those days he was just a laddie, red-haired like myself and freckle-faced. Ferny-tickles, Jessie called the freckles. Passionately addicted to all outdoor pursuits, he became known as the sporting parson, and had won trophies for running, hurdling, and high jumping. He played cricket, tennis, golf, was a crack shot and a friend of the famous athlete, Eric Liddell, his great hero.

'Sport daft!' Jessie called him.

If he was home for the weekend he changed into his plus fours, and he and Father would go off to see the local rugby team – Jedforest – play Hawick or Kelso. I was left behind to assuage their ravenous appetites when they came back clamouring for bacon and eggs. They sat at the table replaying every move of the match. Why had Rutherford held on to the ball so long? He should have kicked for touch or tried an up and under. The referee was rotten!

'More tea, please,' or 'Pass the butter,' was all they said to me.

Afterwards my brother would go out and knock a golf ball in the field as a little recreation. It would never occur to him to offer to clear the table or help to wash the dishes. That was women's work.

He and the other divinity students whom he brought to the farm at weekends had a fetish for keeping fit, which frequently ended in disaster. I was sometimes allowed to field for them or retrieve their cricket balls; and looked on in awe while they swung dumbells in the kitchen at night and examined each other's biceps.

I remember one lanky youth, newly ordained and destined to become a missionary in the foreign field, coming a cropper when he fell off a vaulting horse which they had set up in the steading. We had some difficulty stemming the blood and patching up his nose to make him look holy enough to appear in the pulpit next day when he was due to preach in Jedburgh. We all sat in the back pew and gazed at him apprehensively while he addressed the Lord and dabbed at his damaged neb with a borrowed handkie.

Sometimes I had difficulty sorting out the sacred from the secular. They were all just daft laddies at heart, whether they had heard the call or not.

Yet, when he was dressed up in his dog collar and good blacks, my brother could look the part of a proper preacher, though to Jessie he was still a callant. 'Have ye weshed ahint your lugs?' she would ask him.

Mother was pleased to have a minister in the family. It was a kind of status symbol, a stepping stone to heaven. Her son would get us all in and ensure that we had comfortable front seats. 'My boy, the minister,' she referred to him proudly, and tried not to call him Sonny as she had done in the past. His real name was Henry John, abbreviated to H.J. in the family. But it was a great satisfaction to her when she heard his parishioners refer to him as 'the minister' or even His Reverence. Her Sonny whom she had nursed through the mumps and the measles.

Father was better at hiding his feelings. I think he felt a trifle embarrassed at being closely related to someone so intimate with God. He had a great fund of comic stories about ministers, but now with one in the family he felt he had to curb his funny bone in his son's presence. Indeed, we all had to be a bit more circumspect. It was a solemn state, being connected with a minister of the kirk.

There was not only the kirk to think about. There was the Manse. His Reverence could not inhabit an ordinary dwelling place. He had to be housed in an edifice fit for his standing in the community, a miniature house of God. Miniature! Anything but that. Most Manses were vast buildings with dozens of draughty rooms, long passages leading to inconvenient kitchens; attics, cellars, outhouses, glebes, and a garden that would have kept Adam occupied from dawn till dusk.

The size was supposed to compensate for the pittance paid to the preacher. (Less than £300 a year, I think, in my brother's case.) In bygone days when ministers had quiverfuls of hungry bairns to feed, they eked out their meagre stipends by cultivating the glebe and by keeping sheep, hens and pigs. Scythes and spades were as often in their hands as the Good Book.

In my brother's time the big Manses were more of a burden than a blessing. Heating the house and furnishing it, however sparsely, was a drain on the privy purse. Curtains had to be put up on all windows 'for the look of the thing!' Hospitality must be handed out to all-comers who expected the Manse to have an ever open door, and often taxed the minister's faith that the Lord would provide. No matter how frugal his own fare, he must be willing to share it with all droppers-in. It was a heavy burden to carry.

Where would any overwrought minister have been without a helpmate to ease his load? A Lady of the Manse was an essential adjunct, almost as important in the parish as His Reverence himself.

I often wondered how ministers chose their long-suffering partners. Did they catechise a likely candidate with a spate of pertinent questions? 'Can you make ends meet? Run the Women's Guild? Play the organ? Open bazaars? Weed the garden? Go round with a collecting

14

book? Visit the sick? Be *nice* to everybody? Make do and mend? Never have a spare penny to spend on yourself?' If she said yes he dragged her off to the altar knowing he had secured a willing horse to share his shackles.

It was no easy task being mistress of a Manse, the focus of every critical eye in the parish. The minister had spent years training for his job, but his wife had to learn by trial and error. And she could make or mar him in the eyes of the congregation. '*He*'s all right. Preaches a good sermon. But *her*! Far too stuck-up. Forbye, she can't bake a good scone or put up a prayer at the Guild!' It could be the other way round, and the Lady of the Manse by pouring oil on troubled waters could smoothe away countless difficulties for her husband. 'The minister's no great shakes. Can't preach for toffee. But his wife's such a nice wee wumman. She *listens* to you and you always get a warm welcome at the Manse. And a good tea.'

But what if the minister were not married? My brother was a bachelor, not only of divinity. 'Ower young to mairry yet.' So who was to fill the role of Lady of the Manse?

I had been aware of confabs going on behind closed doors but I did not know the outcome till I received a letter postmarked Edinburgh from His Reverence himself. Fancy him writing to me! He was not asking me, just telling me what had been decided. That I should come and housekeep for him, acting as Lady of the Manse till he found a proper lady to take my place. In the meantime, I could be preparing myself for the task, learning a bit more about cookery and what duties I would have to perform. It would be something for me to do. He was sure we would get on fine. Your loving brother, H.J.

Something for me to do!

True enough, I had no trade. I was not even educated beyond the confines of Jedburgh Grammar School where

I had passed my exams – the Highers – creditably enough to gain entrance to a college in Edinburgh. The next step would be the university and then . . . Man proposes. God disposed that I should fall ill with rheumatic fever before I could take my place in George Watson's Ladies College, where my elder sister had gone to be turned into a lady. Now she, too, was far above me in superiority, capped and gowned at the university and pursuing her own career.

There was a long convalescence after which I had not the strength of will to fight for my own destiny. My parents decided I had better just stay at home and be useful. I could help milk the cows, churn the butter, wash the dishes, clean the house, gather in the eggs, and generally act as extra slavey. Unpaid, of course. What would I need money for? I was fed, clothed and housed.

It was my brain that was not getting enough nourishment, but I was content enough to drift through the days, for I had my own secret outlet. Whenever I could escape from household chores I retired to my bedroom or to the ruined castle on the hill to write my stories. When I was not writing I was reading. Anything I could lay my hungry eyes on: old *Quivers* I found in the garret, tattered volumes of Sir Walter Scott, the Bible which I read from Genesis to Revelations, even *Inquire Within Upon Everything*. Any book I could beg or borrow; any book with *words* in it. It was words that mattered most and how to put them together.

It was a hitty-missy way of educating myself. Little wonder there are great gaps in my knowledge, frayed edges which let me down to this day.

But at least I was getting occasional 'pieces' accepted. Homespun articles describing life on a farm. My first was about a harvest-home (a *kirn*, we called it in the Borders). Not only was it published under my initials in an

Edinburgh evening paper, but they paid me for it with a postal order for a guinea. One pound, one shilling. So I was worth *something*. I sent stories, too, to the BBC's 'Children's Hour' which sometimes brought in another guinea.

I looked more eagerly for the postie every day. He brought rejections more often than acceptances, but I kept on trying. I had staying power, if nothing else. One day I would write a book. If I was left to my own resources I would just write and write, read and read.

Jessie used to dunt me back to reality. 'Ye're awa' in a dwam again, lassie. What are ye thinkin' aboot?'

'I was just wondering,' I said guiltily. There were so many things to wonder about.

I wondered if other folk ever wondered? They all went about, it seemed, with closed faces. Were they shutting the door on hopes, doubts, fears, hiding their flights of fancy behind matter-of-fact façades?

The trouble was I had no one to discuss *ideas* with, silly though mine often were. Sometimes Father had a faraway look in his eyes. Was he seeing himself in a different role from that of a farmer? An entertainer on the stage, perhaps. Did Mother when she keeked in the little kitchen mirror sometimes see herself young and beautiful, the belle of the ball?

And what about Jessie telling me briskly, 'Stop dawdlin', lassie. It'll no' mend the bairn's breeks.' Did she never wonder how the sky stayed up or what her life would have been like if she had been born a Duke's daughter?

'No!' she told me flatly when I ventured to ask her. 'What I'm wonderin' is how ye'll get on in a Manse. A glaiket lassie like you.'

Glaiket means daft, but how could I suddenly become sensible?

'I'll just have to try,' I sighed.

2. Pilgrim's Progress

The first thing to do was get rid of my pigtails.

Whoever heard of a Lady of the Manse with two plaits of ginger hair swinging over her shoulders? Jessie used to tell me I had the thickest head in the Borders. It was her own fault for singeing the ends till the hair sprouted in all directions and I looked like a toozy oobit, she told me. I knew that toozy meant tousled. 'But what's an oobit?' I asked her. She had no idea; it was just an expression. But I found out for myself that an oobit was a hairy caterpillar. So that was what I looked like!

I tried putting it up to make me look more sedate, but it just tumbled down again no matter how I tried to anchor it with strong hairpins. So I decided there was nothing else for it but to cut off the pigtails.

It would be easy enough. I wanted to do it myself with the kitchen scissors. Snip-snap! and that would be the end of my worries. Or Jock-the-herd could do it with the clipping shears, the way he cropped the men's shaggy locks when they became overgrown. 'Mind ma lugs!' they protested when he drew blood; but it would be worth a little pain, I felt, to get rid of my encumbrance.

Mother would not hear of it. 'You'll have to go to a real hairdresser. Your father's barber in Jedburgh'll do it for you.'

The barber took one look at my hair and said, 'Dodsakes, lassie ye've got the thickest heid . . .'

'Yes, I know. Cut it off,' I urged him.

'Your heid?' said he, giving me a pawky look. 'Haud on till I sherpen ma shears.'

It didn't hurt a bit. He never even drew blood. But it was kind of sad to see the pigtails lying on the floor, poor things, looking lost and lonely. 'D'ye want to tak' them hame as souvenirs?' the barber asked compassionately.

I shook my head, then shook it again in surprise at feeling so light-headed. The barber was looking at me appraisingly. 'Ye were a wee lassie when ye came in,' he said, sweeping away the discarded pigtails.

'What am I now?' I asked apprehensively.

'Mair like a wee laddie.'

Mercy! What would my brother's parishioners make of *that*?

The trouble with my bobbed hair was its bushiness. I tried plastering it down with water or with Father's hair oil but I was still a toozy oobit. Och well! Nobody would notice me, I hoped. They would be too busy watching their new minister. He was the one who had been ordained, not me.

And indeed it was not a comment about my hair that I overheard on my first appearance in public. It was about my head. Eavesdroppers occasionally hear good of themselves. It was during the induction ceremony that I heard one woman whisper to another, 'She looks awful young, the minister's sister, but she'll do all right. She's got her head screwed on.'

Fancy that! Jessie would be pleased. *She* was the one who had screwed it on.

The induction was terrible. It was a kind of installation ceremony during which all the ministers of the presbytery gathered round my brother like black crows for the 'laying on of hands'. They blessed him, they prayed over him, they presented him with new robes, they made long solemn speeches and called upon God to guide his footsteps. The Lord bless thee and keep thee . . .

I sat like a prisoner in the Manse pew (shut in by my gaoler, the beadle) and tried to keep a reverent look on my face, thinking the longest day must come to an end. It was to be my prison for many a month of Sundays, a square box-pew with a solid table in the middle and cushioned benches all the way round to accommodate the minister's family. But there was only me. There were times when I would have welcomed even a kirk moose for company. It had a musty smell of mothballs and ancient hymn books. Abandon hope all ye that enter in.

At the induction I shared it with my parents who had come to see their son's triumphant entry into his new kirk. Mother was wearing her best hat and beaming proudly at Sonny. She looked every inch the minister's mother. Father was looking at his hands. I could not guess what *he* was thinking. I tried to retreat into one of my dwams, as Jessie called my daydreams. But I knew fine everyone was staring. I could almost hear Jessie saying sharply. 'Keep your shouthers back an' your heid up!'

Suddenly it was all over and the black crows became human beings, laughing and joking in the church hall while the ladies of the Guild dispensed tea, sandwiches and homemade cakes; and I was introduced to everybody. The minister's sister. They were all very kind and welcoming.

I was bombarded with invitations to come to tea, join the Guild, do the flowers for the church, take a Sunday school class, visit the school, run the Brownies . . . and: 'Can you play the piano?'

'Kind of.'

They all had names and designations but it was difficult to sort them out. 'This is the treasurer . . . the organist . . . the chief elder . . . the chief elder's wife . . . the doctor . . . the doctor's wife . . .'

I made sensible comments when I could, but mostly I just listened; and that was when I heard the comment about my head being screwed on. Maybe that was the trick. Keep quiet and let *them* talk, then perhaps they would not notice my shortcomings.

One benevolent old minister patted me on the head and said, 'There, there!' I knew fine what he meant and gave him a grateful look. The longest day *would* come to an end.

It was not till next morning when Father and Mother drove away in the rattletrap and my brother shut himself into the study that I realized I was alone on a desert island. Father and Mother were going home to the familiar farmhouse. They would soon be seeing Jessie and Jock-the-herd. Where was my home now? Here in this great barn of a Manse. There was a lump in my throat as I turned on the doorstep and walked in to my new domain.

I was used to big houses. I had been born in one, and most of my friends lived in rambling old farmhouses, so I was accustomed to drawing rooms, dining rooms, upstairs and down; but these were homes filled with bustling families. Here, I felt like a pea rattling in a pod, partly because the rooms were so sparsely furnished.

Goodness knows how we had managed to furnish

them at all. The first priority had been to hang curtains at every window to make a brave show. Mother and Jessie had run them up on the creaky sewing machine at home from odds and ends of material. As for furniture, some familiar pieces had been filched from the farmhouse. Even the garret had been raided for discarded chairs, old fire irons, pots, pans, and rugs. Father, who was a compulsive attender of sales (*roups*, they were called in the Borders) had gone round the countryside accumulating carpets, beds, tables and wardrobes, even a grand piano. So in the end every room was 'furnished' after a fashion; but what the Manse lacked most was a lived-in look.

I wandered through some of the rooms, trying to make friends with them.

Downstairs there was the morning room where we would have breakfast in days to come. We used it for little else except the odd meal. Heating, of course, being the problem. The large dining room had only a vast table and sideboard in it. My brother's study, with an open fire, was the cosiest of the lot. A mixture of schoolboy den and holy sanctuary, with a cricket bat and golf clubs in one corner, and his discarded dog collar lying beside an open bible on a chair. His music stand stood at the ready so that he could solace himself by 'scartin' on the fiddle' in moments of stress.

Sermon paper was strewn on the desk covered with scraggly writing only he could decipher. His illegibility, he declared, was the result of hastily taking down notes at lectures when he was a student. And since he was new to the game and had not accumulated a backlog of sermons, he had to start from scratch. No dipping into the bottom of the barrel for him. Even in the bookcase the sacred and secular mingled, theological volumes leaning against *Robin Hood, Hereward the Wake* and the *Boys' Adventure Annual*.

The drawing room was upstairs with the best carpet on the floor, the grand piano, a twirly piano stool, an odd sofa and some unconnected chairs, footstools and small tables. Father had purchased some old paintings, not as good, I thought, as the pictures on the sheep-dip calendar in the kitchen at home, but at least they helped to hide the faded wallpaper. I liked the view of Jedburgh Abbey best and wished I had a photograph of Jessie to set on the piano.

This was the room I tried to keep shipshape so that I could usher unexpected visitors into it before speeding down to warn H.J. 'I'll just see if the minister's in,' I lied, knowing full well he was practising putting shots on the study carpet. How often I was to climb sedately up those stairs, then slide back down the bannisters, and pop my head round the study door. 'Hurry! It's Mr What's-His-Name, the elder. Put on your dog collar.'

The bedrooms, bathroom and odd boxrooms were all on this floor. The spare room held an outsize bed with brass railings round it and knobs at each corner. They had an infuriating habit of falling off and rolling under the bed. They had to be retrieved, polished now and again, and fixed back on; but only when overnight visitors were expected. Otherwise they got a lick and a promise.

That bed! It provided a resting place for visiting ministers of all shapes and sizes, for divinity students, and once for a wee missionary woman who slept still as a mouse in one corner and scarcely ruffled the sheets.

How I hated the sheets! Monsters which Mother had acquired for her bottom drawer. Part of her 'doon-sittin' '. I always got entangled in them when making up the bed, and was worn out by the time I had battled with giant bolsters, pillowslips, blankets, coverlets, and finally – what a relief – a patchwork quilt to spread on top.

The other bedrooms were all nondescript. The minister's was recognizable because of his sporting trophies on the mantelpiece, and photographs of himself in cricket garb, in running shorts, and one taken in the university quadrangle after his capping ceremony. The only new thing was a dressing gown Mother had made for him, hanging on a hook behind the door. His slippers by the bedside were down at heel. He kept a better pair in the study and slipped his feet into them in moments of ease. There was a Testament on the rickety bedside table and a sports paper lying on the floor. I had a feeling he found more solace from *it* before laying himself down to sleep.

My own room was just a room looking out on the back green, but at least it had a door that shut, and how thankfully I closed it when each long day came to an end. In the morning there never seemed to be time to make the bed. I just flung back the bedclothes and threw myself into it at night. But there was always a bedside book and a jotter at hand. No matter how late or how weary, I would read and scribble to take the day's taste out of my mouth. Sometimes I heard the early birds twittering before I guiltily put out the light and turned on my pillow.

It was downstairs in the back premises that most of my activities took place, and I was soon to discover – the Manse being an open house – how seldom I could get a single job done without interruption. While someone was rapping at the back door another was ringing at the front. I used to run like a hare along passages trying to solve the problem of being in two places at once, often with my hands covered with flour and conscious of the soup boiling over on the range.

There was a row of rusty bells hanging on the kitchen wall which no one ever rang (thank goodness) or answered, left over from a more leisured era. They were marked dining room, drawing room, morning room, master bedroom, even the bathroom. I once rang the drawing room one just for fun. It caused such a commotion that the minister rushed upstairs shedding his slippers on the way. I had no idea it would make such a dirdum. The front doorbell was bad enough. It reverberated through the house and was still ringing by the time I answered the door.

Everything in the back premises was so unhandy that I could have sat down and grat if I had been the bubbling type. The range, for example, was enough to make anyone weep. A temperamental monster invented by the devil. I called it the beezer, and other things. Getting it lit to begin with would have tried the patience of all the saints. And once lit, the beezer belched out great gusts of smoke, roared like a demented demon on windy days, and had a habit of dying away if I turned my back on it. But it had to be given constant attention for it was the only means of heating the bathwater.

Water! I had always taken it for granted. One just turned on the tap and out it flowed. We had pure clear water at home from a spring on the hill. Icy cold. Everyone remarked on its quality. 'Tastes like nectar,' I remember a visitor once saying. I had to look up the word in a dictionary to find out its meaning. Fancy being able to drink like the gods out of a kitchen tumbler!

But that was in a different world. Compared with hilly Roxburghshire, Berwickshire was a flat county where water did not flow freely. It had to be coaxed into the taps by whirligigs – miniature windmills set up at intervals in the fields. Often when we turned on the tap only a trickle came out. Then it was all hands – mostly mine – to man the pump.

The pump in the back kitchen was a beezer with a

capital B. I was used to turning the handle of a churn at home and could lull myself into a kind of stupefied rhythm when working it round and round. The stiff pump required an up-and-down action. Above all it needed stamina. I can recall counting eighty-seven exhausting up and downs before there was sufficient water in the tank for a bath, after which I was too weary to mount the stairs to the bathroom.

To do him justice, the minster helped to 'ca' the haunle', if he had time. It was good for his biceps. As for me, I sometimes kicked the Beezer as I went past it. It did not help the flow of water but it relieved my feelings.

As I wandered into the kitchen I wondered if Jessie was missing me. I was certainly missing her and her helping hands. Not that I didn't have a pair of hands waiting for me in the kitchen attached to a lackadaisical servant-lassie whom I had inherited from the last incumbents. Strangely enough, another brother-and-sister team, but the exact opposite from us. Elderly, staid; above all perjink. The minister had died full of years and his sister had departed to live in Edinburgh, leaving behind a pair of bellows, a drugget carpet, and Euphemia. She was to be paid a pittance and inhabit a wee room off the kitchen. The servant's bedroom.

Euphemia! 'Ye can ca' me Ep,' she told me. Never am I likely to forget her. Her! The minister could never bring himself to call her Euphemia or Ep, just Her!, and never actually came face to face with her if he could help it. He would poke his head round the door to see if the coast was clear and hiss, 'Would you ask Her what she has done with my shoes?' He was always mislaying his footwear.

On one awful occasion I had to purloin his shoes myself in a hurry-scurry when I was forced to take over the part of a policeman in the 'Dramatic'. When I came on stage hanging on to my moustache I could see the minister sitting in the front row in his sandshoes and hear his horrified gasp, 'So *that*'s where they went!' It nearly put me off my lines.

The minister could say what he liked to me but he was never brave enough to confront Ep. I have to admit I never liked her myself. She had a sleekit look about her. Nothing straightforward. Her greatest gift was standing still like a knotless thread, doing nothing. She did not even bother to speak if she could avoid it. 'Nuh!' which I assumed meant no. 'Right-o!' which was a kind of reluctant yes. Jessie would have sorted her out in two toots.

Euphemia sized me up as soon as she set eyes on me. I could almost hear her brain ticking. '*She*'s a soft mark. I'll soon get the better of *her*.' But I got the measure of Ep, too. And because I didn't like her, I was extra polite when asking her to do anything. In any case, I hated giving orders. Fancy a young chit like me telling anyone what to do. 'Euphemia, I wonder if you would kindly go and polish the front door brasses, please?'

'Right-o, miss!' with a long-suffering sigh. Ep sighed a lot. So did I behind her back. If she showed too much reluctance I would say, 'Oh never mind, I'll just do it myself.' Whereupon Ep would sigh and scurry into the refuge of her wee room.

A great deal of scurrying went on in the Manse one way and another; but though Ep was so fushionless she was better than nobody. She couldn't cook. 'Nuh!' But at least she could do a bit of dusting and get the oose from under the beds. 'Right-o!' And she could answer the door if I pushed her in the right direction. 'Take whoever it is into the morning room or up to the drawing room, not straight into the study.' 'Nuh!' 'Tell them the minister'll see them in a minute.' 'Right-o!'

It was always something.

I was to be Martha and Mary rolled into one; much more Martha than Mary. And as time went by my skin hardened. When a visiting missionary went down on his knees in the study and said reverently, 'We'll just put up a prayer,' I emulated Ep by saying 'Right-o! you go ahead. I'll just away and sort the stew.'

God would have to make His own judgement.

3. The Village

'What's happened since I've been away?'

'Naething,' said Jessie, 'except the coo's calved.'

'What colour?' I asked eagerly.

'Black an' white.'

A black-and-white calf! That was news worth hearing. More important than anything happening in a Berwickshire Manse.

It was my first visit home. I had to remember I had two homes now but this was the real one. Overton Bush, which was as much part of me as my little pinky.

There were no free weekends in the God-business, as a minister once put it, so we had to snatch a couple of weekdays from the treadmill, fling a few belongings into the Baby Austin and drive off towards the Cheviots. Begone dull care!

The Baby was a boneshaker like Father's motor, but lighter and easier to push when it broke down. In the right mood it rattled merrily along the road and saved my brother a great deal of legwork when visiting his flock; but often I refused a lift and said, 'I'll just walk,' to avoid the strain of helping to change tyres. I was fed up with holding spanners and trying to heave the Baby out of a ditch. Shank's pownie never let me down.

But today I was eager enough to risk punctures, defective steering, even the dread of the mysterious big end giving way. 'Keep going!' I urged the Baby as we set off on the winding road home. The car responded by gathering speed as the minister, wearing a cloth cap pushed down over his eyes – a hooker-doon – honked the horn and whirled round corners as if competing in a race. Soon we would leave the flat lands behind and get our first glimpse of the hills of home.

> And see ye not that bonny road
> That winds aboot the ferny brae?
> That is the road to far elfland
> Where you and I maun gae.

When the road became steeper I shoogled backwards and forwards as Father did when helping Tin Lizzie to mount the hills. 'Keep going, Baby! Keep going!' Kelso! We scooshed through the Square, over the bridge, along beside the Tweed with a lovely glimpse of Floors Castle. The back road towards Oxnam was the quickest way home, so we took that and soon had a first sight of the farmhouse across the fields.

There was a lump in my throat. 'You're a softie!' I told myself, but the lump was still there when we reached the road end and turned into the bumpy farm track. The last lap.

The Baby danced over the rough ruts as if scenting the stable, past the gean tree, past the crab apples, past the cottages. Mrs Thing was out shaking her rug. I waved wildly to her, shaking off my own dust. My brother tooted his horn to scatter the cocks and hens out of the way, then as if breaking the tape, he drew up at the kitchen door. We had made it.

Jessie was standing there with a pail in her hand. What better welcome could I want? If she was pleased to see me, she didn't show it, but that was Jessie. 'Ye're back, lassie!'

Yes, I was back.

The minister at once reverted to Sonny and sat in the parlour regaling his proud parents with tales of his prowess in the parish; but I wanted to get away from all that, to run about and kick up my heels like a pony set free. I shed my cares chasing the bubblyjock, I swung on a gate, I climbed the big tree and tore a hole in my stockings before galloping off to look at the black-and-white calf.

Jock-the-herd called to me. 'Man-lassie, ye're loupin' aboot like a loose.' (A loose, I knew, was a louse.) 'Ye've no' improved.' I think he was glad I hadn't.

'How are you, Jock?'

'Fine.'

Everything was fine. Presently Sonny came out in his shorts to practise the long jump. A blessing the brethren could not see him now with his tousled hair and a torn semmit, and I went in to help Jessie with the kirning.

It was easy turning the handle of the churn compared with that diabolical pump at the Manse. Easy to get into a measured rhythm, slow and steady at the start. 'The Lord's My Shepherd.' 'Pop Goes the Weasel' was fine for a speed up later on. Then we heard the thud-thud of the butter. Back to the slow movement. 'O God of Bethel'.

I was drinking a tumbler of buttermilk, which Jessie called soor dook, when she asked me a question. 'Tell me, lassie, hoo are ye gettin' on doonbye?'

Doonbye! Away in a different world.

'Fine,' I said, taking the easy way out.

But it was not really true. There were a hundred things to tell her, not all of them 'fine', but somehow I could not find the words nor see my new life clearly enough to talk about it yet. The picture was too blurred. I would have to wait till I could sharpen it into focus.

I told her a bit about the Manse, my struggles with the water supply, about Ep. 'Set her up!' Jessie tightened her lips. 'I'd sort her!'

'Oh! I wish you would,' I thought, wiping away my buttermilk moustache. What a difference it would make to have Jessie in the Manse kitchen. But there were other places, too, where things were not always 'fine'. Sometimes my duties took me out and about in the Village.

The Village was the name everyone called my brother's parish, though it spread far beyond the Village itself; but the focal point was a long straggling street with the Manse at the top, the church halfway down, a railway station, shops, an inn, and a cattle market at the foot. More like a town to me than a village. At the bottom a winding road joined the Great North Road which ran parallel to the Village, the busy highway leading to Edinburgh in one direction and Berwick in the other.

I was used to living on a frontier, not to such bustle. From the Manse windows I could see the traffic on the Great North Road. It was never empty, always a van, a lorry, a car or a motor bicycle coming or going. And nearer at hand I could see people passing by the Manse. *They* were a new breed to me, for no one ever passed by the farmhouse at home. There was nowhere else to go; it was the end of the line.

Here, people came and went all the time, some walking, some on bicycles, some in cars. Up the road, past the schoolhouse, past the rectory where the Pisky Parson lived, away up to territory as yet unknown to me. Some, far too many, did not pass by at all. When I heard the click of the gate I hastily took off my apron and thought, 'Help! Not again!' before the bell announced another caller on the doorstep.

They came in shoals at first, to bid us welcome, to consult the minister, to invite us to visit *them*, to leave their cards. It was a mixed parish – commoners and gentry – and it was the gentry who left their cards on the hall table, several for each family. It would take me ages to sort out who was who. Any stranger who called at our lonely farmhouse in the Cheviots, even a tramp, was a welcome diversion, but at the Manse I had more than my fill. 'Shut up!' I used to scold the noisy doorbell. 'Give me a minute's peace!'

When I had to go down the Village street, maybe on a mission of mercy or just to buy a pan loaf at the baker's, I was aware of keekers from behind every curtain. 'That's her! The minister's sister!' I straightened my shoulders and walked sedately. No leaping about like a louse for the Lady of the Manse. And no darting out of the door in an old jumper and skirt, with my hair on end. It was a struggle trying to be neatly dressed at all times, especially with my limited wardrobe.

I had two decent outfits: my good costume made by the tailor in Jedburgh – brown with sensible shoes to match – and my Harris tweed coat with leather buttons and a green hat to go with it. The hat was just a hat, the coat of such everlasting quality that it would never wear out. When I got caught in a shower of rain it smelt of peat and heather. I longed for something more dashing, a scarlet cloak, maybe; but because of my red hair I had always been dressed in browns, greens, and blues. The great thing was not to look too conspicuous. 'And remember always to wear gloves,' my mother had cautioned me. So I did my best to look perjink and blend into the background.

The men doffed their hats to me but I was used to that. Father and his friends were all great doffers; it was the done thing. I bowed as graciously as I could, hoping that would be enough and I could pass by. But often they would cross the road to shake hands and say kind words to which I would reply, 'Oh yes, thank you. Everything's fine and the minister's well.' Mr This and That put their hats back on their heads and went their ways. What did they make of me, I wondered? Occasionally there would be a jokey one who patted me on the back and said, 'Now if you're in any trouble, just send for me. I'm your man!' 'Oh yes, I will, thank you.'

It was difficult to curb my spirits when I met some bairns kicking a ball up the street or hitting out at each other with their schoolbags; or running with a gird and cleek as I used to do at home. I longed to join in the fun, and once I forgot myself to the extent of kicking the ball back to them.

'Jings!' I heard a wee laddie gasp. 'Fancy *her* up at the Manse kickin' a ball!'

The only other village I had known was Camptown, a mile from the farmhouse at home, but it was only half-a-dozen houses with Bella's post office shop in the middle. Not a village with a capital V. Yet I often thought longingly of Bella and wished I could pop into her shop, which was only a but-and-ben, though she stocked everything from stays and jotters to pandrops and pirns.

For long enough I had thought Bella's name was the one above the shop, printed in faded letters. CONFECTIONARY. As a child I had no idea what the word meant or that the spelling was wrong. She was Bella Confectionary, as far as I was concerned, as good a name as any.

On my first walk down the Village street I discovered a real confectioner's with a window full of mouthwatering goodies. How could I pass by without gawping at the bottles of coloured sweets, the macaroon bars, chocolate whirls, peppermint creams, homemade tablet and Berwick cockles? There were familiar items, too, such as Bella stocked. Sherbet, liquorice, jujubes, dolly mixtures, even Jethart snails.

I was so absorbed I had forgotten where I was till I saw a hand beckoning me in, an old gnarled hand twisted with rheumatism, making insistent motions for me to enter. So I had to open the door and set the bell tinkling.

'I – I was just looking,' I said uneasily, for I had no spare money in my purse to indulge in sweetmeats.

'Ay, an' I was lookin' at you,' said the old woman seated behind the counter. 'I canna get up wi' ma bad legs. Arthuritis. But I just wanted to say welcome to the Village. Shake hands, lassie.'

I shook her hand carefully for I was afraid I might hurt it. My heart warmed to her, for she had called me lassie. It made me feel like a human being again. Sarah was her name, she told me. Sarah Googly: a strange name, I thought, yet no stranger than Bella Confectionary.

When I called her Mrs Googly she shook her head. '*Miss* Googly, but ye can ca' me Sarah. I'm a spinster.'

'So am I,' I confessed.

But Sarah was one up on me. 'I've got a daughter,' she confided. 'Kate.'

A love child, I jaloused. There was nothing in that. I had gone to the local school with many whose mothers were unwed. They were no different from the rest of us; all Jock Tamson's bairns.

Sarah went on to tell me about her daughter. (Not about the father: I never learnt about *that*. She seemed very proud of her, particularly that *she* was respectably married. 'Mistress Niven. Her man's one o' your brother's elders. Maister George Niven, an awful fine fella.'

They all lived together. The Nivens kept the General Store 'ben the hoose' and Sarah was in charge of the confectionery. She managed fine. The customers helped her to unscrew the lids of the sweetie bottles and to break the toffee with a little hammer.

'I'm a lucky wumman,' she kept telling me, though now and again she shifted her position and stifled an exclamation of pain. 'Eh whowh!'

It brought back memories of Jessie when thumping her stomach during bouts of the bile. 'Eh whowh!' It was a kind of painkiller.

'It's just a stoond,' said Sarah. As she talked on, I listened, the one thing I was good at, and we were getting on a treat when her daughter, Mistress Niven, came along the passage from the General Store. She looked put out when she saw me and heard her mother talking so familiarly with the Manse 'lady'. She was different from her mother, small and nippy, far more perjink than I was, and anxious to make a good impression.

'Oh my! What a shame! You've not even sat down. Can I not get you a cup of tea?'

'No! No thanks, Mrs Niven. I just popped in . . .'

'Well, you'll come properly the next time and have your tea in the parlour.' With wee crocheted doyleys on the plates, the best teacups and the sugar tongs brought out.

'Oh yes, I will, thank you.'

Old Sarah was deftly twisting a paper poke with her rheumaticky hands, into which she shovelled some treacle toffee. 'Something for ye to sook, lassie. Tell the meenister to ca' in. I'd like a crack wi' him aboot the

Bible.' She knew the Good Book inside out, she had told me, and liked to study it, but her bad legs would not carry her to the kirk on Sundays.

'I'll tell him,' I promised and went off sucking a lump of toffee, thankful that I had found at least one friend in the Village. I had a feeling old Sarah could have preached as good a sermon as my brother any Sunday.

Though, to give him his due, Sonny was pulling out all the stops and making a good impression on the congregation who turned out in great force on the Sabbath to hear his discourse. Not just because he was 'the new meenister'. Every able-bodied parishioner went to the kirk – they had been brought up to it, like supping their porridge – and if there was a gap in the pews it was noted. 'Mrs Cowan's missin', an elder would say with a worried frown. 'I'd better ca' in an' see what's up.'

My brother moiled and toiled in the study over his sermons, with occasional bursts of fiddle music in between. He never discussed them with me, of course; and as I sat imprisoned in my box-pew I tried to guess whether the text would be taken from the first reading or the second.

'My text for today,' H.J. would announce solemnly, 'comes from Job Chapter 19, verse 2. How long will ye vex my soul and break me in pieces with words?'

Mercy! What is he going to make of *that*, I wondered?

I tried to listen dutifully though it was difficult to concentrate with so many of my own thoughts whirling through my head. Difficult, too, not to sag. 'Sit up straight,' I scolded myself. 'Folk are watching.' But I was watching, too, out of the corner of my eye, trying to sort out who was who and to turn them into real people.

When the minister put up a prayer they all reacted in different ways. No bending the knees in a Scots kirk. The gentry leant forward and buried their heads in their gloved hands. The lower orders just shut their eyes and screwed up their faces, trying not to gant. (To yawn). I sometimes keeked through my fingers when H.J. was addressing the deity, and sometimes addressed Him myself. 'O God, I wonder if I put too much salt in that lentil soup? And what on earth can I make for supper tonight? Toad-in-the-hole! A-men!'

Sunday was no day of rest for me. His Reverence shut himself in the study after lunch to look over his sermon for the evening service, or maybe to practise press-ups on the rug. No fiddle music permitted on Sunday. Ep was off for the day, so I had a great deal of rubbing and scrubbing to do in the kitchen, but it would have been sacrilege to hang as much as a dishtowel out in the back garden. I had to stick to the rules. Remember the Sabbath day . . .

But the dreaded doorbell did not take a day off. On one occasion when I went to answer it, drying my hands on my apron, I found a small shilpit laddie trembling with terror on the doorstep. (Shilpit was one of Jessie's words. It meant puny and sickly.)

'I – I want to speak to God,' he gulped.

'Right-o!' I was getting used to Ep's expression. 'I'll just see if he's in,' said I, without blinking an eye.

As I was turning to make my way to the study he called me back. 'Hi, miss!' Then, in a conspiratorial whisper: 'Are ye no' feart livin' wi' *him*?'

'No, I'm not.'

'Fancy!' He gazed at me in astonishment and admiration. 'Ye're terrible brave!'

It was my first meeting with Wee Wullie, but not my last.

Another human being I encountered was the Tattie-Bogle. I discovered him in the Manse garden one day when I wandered out to explore the territory, wondering what lay hidden under the hard earth. We had arrived in the dead of winter and there was no sign of growth, only withered shrubs and stubbly soil. Perhaps hidden treasure was lurking underneath, and come spring the sleeping beauty might awake. Then I would be surprised by the sight of a riot of fragrant flowers.

My first surprise was when I looked up and saw the Tattie-Bogle. He was standing as still as the ones dotted around the farm fields at home, bogles I had helped Jock-the-herd to dress in old duds from the kist in the garret; but they were better clothed than the one in the Manse garden. His coat was in tatters, his ragged breeks were tied round the legs with binder twine, his boots were caked with mud, and his bonnet so battered I would have dumped it in the midden.

I almost jumped out of my skin when I saw smoke coming from his clay pipe. The bogle was alive.

He shuffled from one foot to another when he saw me. 'Canny do muckle in the gairden the noo,' said he, picking up a spade and leaning on it. Then I realized there was something familiar about him. Where had I seen him before? In the kirk on Sunday.

It was Leckie, the beadle, the most important man in the parish next to the minister. More important, in his own opinion.

On Sundays, transformed into a pillar of the kirk, dressed sprucely in black trousers, white collar, and a cutaway coat, he rang the bell, carried the big Bible solemnly up the pulpit stairs, and conducted the minister through from the vestry, as if leading him to his execution. He glared at latecomers, inclined his head to the gentry and shut me into my box-pew with a warning look. 'Sit still and behave yoursel'!' Now here he was, a Tattie-Bogle in the Manse garden.

As time went on I grew accustomed to seeing Leckie

about the place. It appeared that he had a dual personality, doing odd jobs during the week dressed in his old duds, and blossoming out on Sundays as the minister's right-hand man. It was rumoured that he took a bucket in the inn on Saturday nights, but if so his step never faltered on the pulpit stairs, and he looked soberer than the minister himself.

These were things I was just beginning to find out, not yet clear enough in my mind to discuss with Jessie in the farmhouse kitchen. So, as I drained my soor dook I stuck to my story. 'Everything's fine.'

Jessie knew, all the same. She gave me one of her keen glances and said, 'A'weel, stick in, lassie. Ye'll just need to thole it.'

So I did.

After our brief respite we went back to the Manse with half-a-dozen hens and a cockerel in the back of the car. And on my lap a black labrador puppy whom I christened Bush, after Overton Bush. Maybe *he* would help me to thole it.

4. Weathering the Storm

It was not so much a baptism of fire as of frost. Never will I forget that first winter in the Manse.

> The ice was here, the ice was there,
> The ice was all around;
> It cracked and growled and roared and howled
> Like noises in a swound!

I was used to wintry weather on the farm, to being snowed in for weeks on end, with all the miseries that accompanied the storm, and to making the best of a bad job. 'We'll just have to dree oor weirds,' Jessie used to say, which meant we would have to put up with it. What else was there to do?

One day, I remember, when I was trudging over the

41

snow like Lucy Gray on my way to school, I heard a cottage wife squealing like Grumphy the pig. There she was, running barefoot amongst the snowdrifts. Had she taken leave of her senses? No! 'I'm curin' ma chilblains,' she explained, prancing up and down on her bare toes. It seemed a painful remedy, but Mrs Thing declared it did the trick, so I grew accustomed to her squeals every winter. Snow and suffering went together.

But this was different. Misery piled upon misery. The worst storm they had ever experienced in that part of the Borders.

It began on the day His Reverence and I set out to visit Berwick which was to be my 'big toon', as Jedburgh was when I lived on the farm. I was looking forward to crossing the frontier into that other country, England, to exploring the wynds and vennels, the ramparts, the open-air market. I knew Berwick had been the target of many a tug of war between the Scots and the English, that after a tussle the English had tugged harder; and though the town was situated at the mouth of the Tweed – surely the most Scottish of rivers – it was now firmly in the hands of the 'auld enemy' with walled defences around it to keep out the warring Scots.

But we, H.J. and I, were coming in peace to do a little shopping and see the sights.

We did not get far before fate struck the first blow. It was a bitterly cold day and I was thankful for my Harris tweed coat as we set out in the Baby down the Village street, past old Sarah Googly's shop, past the kirk, and out on to the Great North Road. Soon we would reach the small township of Ayton and speed towards the debatable land where we could cross into another country.

We never reached it.

The car was weaving from side to side, squealing as if *it*

had chilblains. Then all of a sudden it spun round on its tracks and faced the way we had come. Luckily there was no lorry on the road to crash into us, so I got out automatically to do my usual pushing, and fell flat on my face. I tried to get up, but down I went again. There was no grip on the road.

The minister let out an ungodly word. It was no go. Goodbye Berwick! The snow was beginning to fall but it was the icy road that was the problem, and how to get the Baby home. There was nothing for it but to dree oor weirds. By dint of much pushing and heaving, we slipped, slithered and limped our way back with no feeling in our fingers and toes. Thankfully we pushed the car into the Manse garage and shut the door. Little did we know it was the last we would see of the Baby for six long weeks. By next morning the garage door was frozen stiff.

So was the pump.

Though this was only the first blow, in a sense it was the last straw, for not only did it mean no hot water, it meant no cold water; indeed no water at all. Though I hated the pump, how willingly I would have worked the handle till my arm ached if only I could have coaxed a trickle from the tap.

The lack of water was bad enough. The lack of heat was worse, for I dared not light the kitchen range in case the boiler burst. And how could I cook?

'Use your rummlegumption,' I admonished myself. There was the study fire. I would just have to cook on that. And so I did, balancing pots on a wee trivet in front, while the minister huddled over it in his overcoat, worrying away at his sermon.

As for water, Leckie the Tattie-Bogle occasionally came to the door with a pailful, and as time went by I helped myself to some of the spectacular icicles hanging like stalactites or mites from the eaves of the outhouses. Meantime the piercing wind whistled through the draughty Manse, sending flurries of snow through every crack and crevice.

'It can't get worse. It can't!' I kept consoling myself. But it did.

Ep was no help at all. She just stood around shivering and sighing, with her shoulders hunched up against the cold. I lent her a pair of woolly gloves, made her bowls of hot soup, and since there were not enough hot-water bottles to go round sacrificed mine and wrapped my freezing feet in an old cardigan at night.

Because I disliked Euphemia so much I went out of my way to be nice to her, trying to cheer her up by giving her some cushions for her dingy little room and a bright coverlet for the bed. No response from Ep. I think she despised me as much as I disliked her. We rubbed each other's fur the wrong way.

It was my fault, I suppose, for not trying to train her properly, but I was not trained myself. Now and again I wound myself up and made a mild protest. One day before the great freeze I came into the kitchen carrying a heavy tray and found Ep leaning listlessly against the table, doing nothing as usual. She was wearing a grubby pinny.

She did not offer to relieve me of my load and for once my dander rose.

'Have you nothing to do, Euphemia?' I asked with an edge to my voice.

'Nuh!'

'Don't you think your apron's a bit dirty?' I ventured.

'Uhuh!'

'Well, why not wash it?' I suggested before running out of steam.

'Right-o!' sighed Ep, untying her apron with little

44

enthusiasm and giving me one of her looks. I was glad I could not hear what she was thinking. It was no use; I would never get anywhere with her.

But still waters run deep. It was during the storm that I made a startling discovery. Ep was not as mim-mou'd as she appeared on the surface. She had a better hot-water bottle than mine.

I had imagined I heard scufflings in the wee room off the kitchen. Could there be mice or even a rat in the servant's bedroom? Then one morning when I came suddenly into the kitchen I saw the rat scuttling from the room and out the back door. A gangling youth with a tousy mop of black hair. Ep came out of the room after him in her bare feet.

'Euphemia!' I gasped. 'Who was that?'

'Naebody.'

'Don't be silly! I saw him. Who is he and what is he doing here?' A silly question.

Ep gave a gulp. 'The windy's stuck,' she mumbled, as if *that* explained everything. For a moment I, too, was stuck. Then I realized that was how he had been getting in, through her bedroom window from the back green. Now, like all the windows in the Manse, it was frozen, so he was forced to use the back door.

'Ye'll no' tell the meenister?' said Ep, shuffling her bare feet. I noticed she had a chilblain on her big toe.

'Will I not?' I said coldly.

'Nuh!' said Ep. 'Dinna!' She was half imploring me, half threatening.

I did not know how to deal with the situation. Who was I to stand in judgement? Yet, I knew I ought to take some action.

'It'll have to stop,' I said severely.

'Right-o!' said Ep, and shuffled back to her room in her bare feet.

So for a while we shared a guilty secret.

I swithered whether to tell the minister or not, but he already had enough problems on his plate. We both had, and one of mine was how to fill the plates. It took all our time, energy, and ingenuity just to survive each day, and to help any who came begging to the door.

Our most constant caller was the old lady who lived with a smelly pug dog for company in a house in the Loaning, the lovers' lane behind the Manse. The pug, wrapped in a woolly comforter, and Bush, our new puppy, hated each other on sight. So a great deal of snapping, barking and yapping went on between them.

I could have barked, too, at old Miss Calder, for I dreaded her visits. She looked like a witch in her hooded cloak, with her bent back, sharp tongue, and clicking teeth. She was miles above me intellectually and let me know it, but adversity is a great leveller. During that severe winter we were all forced to ask for help – even Miss Calder who accepted it with bad grace. It was little enough I had to give her. Soup now and then, hot potatoes baked in the study fire, a can of water, a jug of milk.

I melted icicles for her, split kindling, and escorted her back home, slithering over the ice with the pug snapping at my heels. On the doorstep she would try to detain me by launching into some abstruse subject far above my head.

'I'll have to go, Miss Calder,' I would say, stamping my frozen feet.

'Huh! That's the young!' She clicked her false teeth disapprovingly. 'No time for old folk. No time for conversation . . .'

No time for anything but just getting through the day. 'Stick it out!' I kept telling myself. I had no past, no future, only the present with its icy problems. Even the

46

kirk bell froze for the first time in living memory, but not the Manse doorbell. 'Oh Jessie, help!'

Help was at hand. As time went by, I came to welcome the doorbell's jangle, for it often brought comfort from warm-hearted parishioners, sorry for the young pair marooned in the Manse. Folk I had never seen before thrust gifts into my hand. Scones, butter, potatoes, even a hambone. A pailful of water was a godsend, a can of oil for the lamps another gift from heaven. And the best gift of all was a paraffin heater which we set in the hall to take the edge off the chill air. I had to keep an eye on it, for if it was turned up too high, little black specks went floating through the house, but at least they were a change from white flakes of snow.

Others came offering practical help, not always successful. Mr Sturrock, the strait-laced chief elder, who never smiled or cracked the smallest joke, arrived one day with his customary long face and, surprisingly, a hammer in his hand. I thought by the look of him he had come to do me in, but he marched into the study and did in the window instead. The minister was out on a mission of mercy, so I left Mr Sturrock to it.

I doubt if he had ever used a hammer before – his wife was the handyman in their house – but he attacked the frozen bolt as if he meant business. After a few futile attempts the hammer slipped from his fingers and fell to the floor, but not before cracking one of the large windowpanes to smithereens.

Mr Sturrock's long face grew even longer. 'Never mind,' I said cheerfully, as if pleased to have a blast of freezing air blowing through the study. 'We'll easily patch it up.'

Easily! The best I could do was find a large piece of cardboard, and *that* was a difficult enough job. Then I did the hammering, though I was almost as ham-handed as the elder who held the cardboard in place while I tried to knock in the nails. I hit him on the thumb several times and he went away sucking it, leaving us in semidarkness, colder than ever. But he meant well.

There were times when I went to answer the doorbell and discovered no one there. Only an anonymous gift on the doorstep. Once it was a pheasant left by the gentry. Thanks to Jessie, I knew how to pluck and cook it. I made a savoury stuffing with oatmeal and pot-roasted it on the study fire. Then for once we had a feast, at the end of which His Reverence loosened his waistcoat and breathed, 'I'm fed up!' It was a nice feeling. I would have invited old Miss Calder to share our spoil had not Satan got the better of me; but I took her some soup next day made from the bones.

The back door was as busy as the front. Leckie, the Tattie-Bogle, came with a sack of logs and a shovel with which he tried to scrape a path to the gate. We ran short of coarse salt to sprinkle on it, but I was used to falling down, and came so many croppers I gave up bothering about my bruises. As for dignity, *it* had gone with the icy wind.

The stunted little fellow, Wee Wullie, sometimes called with supplies from Niven's Store where he acted as errand boy. He still persisted in calling my brother God.

'Is he in?' he would ask fearfully, when I answered his knock at the back door.

'No, he's out.'

'That's OK.'

Wee Wullie relaxed and handed over the message-basket. Sometimes I persuaded him to come into the kitchen out of the chill blast, but he never lingered long, looking uneasily over his shoulder in case God suddenly appeared.

'Are you not cold?' I asked him, for he had no overcoat

and his bare knees were blue.

'No, I'm not.' Wee Wullie never complained but went skidding away over the ice. I wished I could do something for him.

The minister went out and about in Wellington boots with a gravat round his neck, doing as much parish work as he could. When he came shivering home he would tell me how cold it was.

'I've noticed!' I said, and made him a hot drink to take the chill off his bones. It was little warmer inside than out.

Meantime things were going on as before in the kitchen where the speeds were dead slow and stop. Ep did a great deal of leaning on the table and hiding her hands under her oxters to keep them warm. Occasionally she stirred her stumps if I prodded her and swept the snow from the back doorstep, but she never instigated anything herself. Except in her bedroom. In spite of my warnings, the rat had returned.

I thought it must be my imagination when I heard the familiar scufflings, but it was all too true. And it was the minister himself who brought it to my attention. He called me into the study one day and shuffled about in his carpet slippers, too embarrassed to look me straight in the face. I wondered what was up and went to steady the pot of stovies cooking on the trivet.

H.J. cleared his throat before coming to the point. 'She'll have to go,' he said, turning away from me.

'Who?' I asked, surprised.

'Her!'

'Oh!' What had he seen or heard? I could not ask him outright but I knew fine what he meant.

'Right-o!' I said. (Ep again!) But who was to bell the cat? 'Will you tell her?'

'No,' said the cowardly minister. 'That's your job.'

'Help! What'll I say?'

'Just say . . .' began H.J. and then stuck. 'Just say she'll have to go and the sooner the better.'

'Right-o!'

But there was nothing Right-o about it. I rehearsed my lines long and hard but never got them off pat; and *I* was the one who blushed with guilt when I finally went into the kitchen to do the dreaded deed. For once Ep was actually doing something. Scraping a burnt porridge pot.

'Leave that, Euphemia. I'll do it myself, after . . .'

After what?

She looked at me in surprise and started to chew her fingers. 'Euphemia,' I began, 'the minister says . . .'

No, that wasn't fair, hiding behind H.J. I started again and said my lines as quickly as I could to get them over and done with. Like swallowing castor oil.

'Euphemia, you've broken your promise. You said you'd behave better and you haven't, so you've got to leave.'

I hung on to the table for support while Ep stopped eating her fingers and gave me one of her strange looks.

'D'ye mean I've got the sack?' she asked.

I nodded. What else was there to say?

Plenty! But it was Euphemia who said it.

Ep, who had never uttered a whole sentence before, now launched into a spate of invective all directed at me. I stood dumbstruck in the direct line of fire listening to her giving me my character. She did not call me an incompetent nincompoop, but that was what she meant. I was soft, silly, daft, not fit for a Manse. I had nae idea how to run a hoose and she was fair scunnered with me.

The awful thing was, every word she said was true. When she stopped I nearly urged her to go on, it was so revealing. But having emptied her gun, Ep burst into floods of tears which rolled like rivulets down her cheeks, then sobbed into her pinny.

'Thank you, Euphemia,' I said quietly and went out into the hall.

I sank down on the bottom step of the stairs, trembling all over. Bush came to lick my hand, then the minister poked his head round the study door. 'Have you done it?' he whispered, as if I had just cut off Ep's head.

I nodded miserably, whereupon he thrust some money into my hand. 'Give Her that,' he said and darted back to his den. That was the end of Ep as far as he was concerned.

I gave Euphemia the money and made sure she had some place to go. Yes! She would bide with Billy. (The rat's family would take her in.) I shook hands with her before she packed her bags and departed.

So now I was left on my own, but at least I got my hot-water bottle back.

5. Wee Wullie

'Soop! Soop! Soop it up!'

The men were prancing on the ice, shouting like excited schoolboys. 'Soop it up! Soop! Soop!' (Which meant 'Sweep! Sweep!') No wonder they called it the Roaring Game.

A pond near the Village had frozen hard enough for the men to bring out their curling stones and sweeping brushes. They were so engrossed in their game, even the intense cold could not curb their enthusiasm. 'Soop! Soop!'

The minister was in the midst of the mêlée, sweeping with the best and putting his heart and soul into it. I wished he would be as energetic with the Manse carpet-sweeper, but that would have been work. Sport was a different matter. After it was over he would come home and sink into a chair, too weary to lift the kettle off the trivet. Here, he could happily heave the weighty curling stone, but at home a duster would be too heavy.

I think the men were quite taken on, seeing him behave like an ordinary mortal. 'Doon here, meenister! Soop! Soop!' Leckie was there, and Mr Sturrock, the long-faced elder. I did not linger long for it was not a ploy for women, but before I left I caught sight of a small shivering laddie lurking in the background. Wee Wullie still without an overcoat. I did not bother to ask if he was cold. He would just have shaken his head.

The next day His Reverence came downstairs from his bedroom dressed in his good blacks and with his dog collar on. He went into the study to search for his bible.

'It's a christening,' he informed me. 'You've been invited so you'd better come.'

'Where?' I asked, untying my apron.

'Somewhere up the Loaning. Hurry and get ready.'

I put on my Harris tweed coat and green hat and slithered after him like an obedient puppy, past old Miss Calder's house, away up the rutted lane till we reached a cottage at the top. It had a dilapidated air about it. 'This must be it.' The minister knocked at the door and settled a solemn expression on his face.

The next moment we were inside a cluttered room where a woman sitting on a sofa struggled to get up. I noticed the stuffing on the sofa was hanging out, the carpet threadbare, and the curtains torn. But the woman seemed unaware of any defects in her surroundings. 'Sit doon, meenister,' she said, not a bit put out. 'Sit doon, miss. We're aye ahint, like the coo's tail!'

Where to sit down was the problem. Everything seemed to be at sixes and sevens. Tapsulteerie, Jessie would have said. I perched on the sofa while the man of the house, half in, half out of his jacket, cleared a chair for the minister. There were various cats, dogs and children scrambling about. And a large lassie holding the new baby in her arms was wiping his face with a dishcloth. It was a homely scene!

Then I noticed a familiar figure hiding below the table. Wee Wullie, too terrified to come out in the presence of God.

It was his baby brother who was to be christened. Hogg, the father, was a fushionless creature, an odd-job man on the railway, easy-osy to the point of laziness, addicted to drink, but good-natured enough.

When a bowl of water was produced for the ceremony he said to my brother, 'A'weel, meenister, ye'll no' mind if the bairn tak's your name?'

How could the meenister mind? He knew it was the custom in country parishes. The first child to be baptized by a new minister had the privilege of taking his name. A proud privilege. 'I'm the meenister's bairn,' the child could boast in later life. Perhaps H.J. had secretly hoped it might be one of the gentry's offspring instead of the smelly baby squirming in his big sister's arms. But we are all God's creatures and he manfully did his duty as earnestly as if he had been dubbing a prince.

'Henry John Hogg I baptize thee, in the name of the Lord.'

And may He have mercy on your soul, I added under my breath.

After blessing the baby who yelled his head off during the entire ceremony – a happy omen, his mother assured us – the minister relaxed over a cup of tea and a stale piece of gingerbread. Hogg, the proud father, was making signals at him, jerking his head and rolling his eyes heavenwards. He had a bottle hidden in the dresser drawer and was inviting His Reverence to wet the baby's head from a cracked tumbler. Meantime, the minister's namesake was receiving succour from another source.

Mrs Hogg had loosened her blouse to reveal nature's taps.

At least it kept Henry John from squealing. During the suckling process Mrs Hogg turned to me and said, 'I hear ye need somebody at the Manse.'

I nodded.

'Ye could have Oor Net, if ye like,' went on Mrs Hogg, indicating the big lassie who was now collecting the teacups. 'She's just oot the school. But she's nae great shakes.'

I was no great shakes myself, so I took a sympathetic look at Nettie. Oor Net. I liked what I saw. There was something soft and pliable about her. With her liquid brown eyes and her shaggy hair, she reminded me of a young calf. I had a feeling we would get on well together, though it would be the blind leading the blind, but somebody was better than nobody. Nettie could go home every evening up the Loaning. So there would be no need to part with my hot-water bottle. And, after all, we were practically related, if not by blood by the minister's name.

It all went flashing through my head while the baby continued to suckle and Wee Wullie to hide under the table. I had a quick conversation with my brother from the corner of my mouth. He was looking a bit desperate by now, hemmed in by Hogg who was trying to refill his glass. 'Yes, go ahead,' he said hurriedly. 'We'll have to be leaving soon.'

So I spoke to Nettie. 'How would you like to come and work in the Manse?'

'Fine,' she said shyly. So it was settled there and then. She would start the next morning.

From the beginning Oor Net and I got on a treat, though it *was* the blind leading the blind. She was willing if not able. I did not anticipate much and she lived up to my expectations; but at least she did not despise me, as Ep had done, and would sympathize with my mistakes just as I overlooked hers.

'O Lord! Ye've went an' forgot to put saut in the kail again. Will I sort it, miss?'

'Right! Go ahead, Nettie.'

We were a fine pair.

Oor Net had a rich store of expletives which some-times slipped out before she could clap her hand to her mouth. They ranged from 'Jings Geordie!' to 'Michty God!', with 'Damnation!' and 'Holy Moses!' in between. Not quite suitable for a Manse, but she tried hard to stifle them, and when dressed in a clean apron and with her hair tethered by a black ribbon, she looked not bad.

The great thing was the minister took to her, or at least accepted her presence, and was not afraid to enter the kitchen and shout, 'Could you find my shoes, please, Nettie.'

The fact that he always pleased and thanked her, gave Oor Net a great boost. She reciprocated by polishing his shoes till they shone like mirrors, and would run and open the front door for him if she saw he was on his way out. She had a habit of falling over her feet. 'Damnation!' she would say, picking herself up. 'O Lord! I hope *he* didn't hear. He's awful human, the meenister,' she would say to me.

'Awful,' I agreed.

But Wee Wullie still kept out of God's way. He came more often to the back door now that his big sister was in residence, bringing groceries from Niven's Store or just hanging about kicking his heels. I sometimes tried to lure him into the kitchen for a hot drink, for he was always shivering and coughing, but even if the minister was out the laddie was reluctant to cross the threshold. I gave him a gravat to wind round his throat – little did he know it was an old Watsonian scarf of my brother's – but what he needed most was a warm overcoat which I could not provide. And some loving care and attention.

Then one day I heard him cough-cough-coughing at the back door. When I went out I found him sitting forlornly on the icy doorstep, looking pitifully thin and ill.

'I'm fine,' he said, trying to rise to his feet. But I made up my mind there and then, and hauled him into the kitchen.

'Nettie,' I said purposefully, 'help me to make up the bed in the wee room. I'm keeping Wullie here till he's better.'

'Jings Geordie!'

'Then you'd better run home and ask your mother if it'll be all right.'

It was all right.

Wee Wullie, past caring what happened to him, meekly allowed himself to be put to bed in the servant's room off the kitchen, clad in one of my warm goonies. Pink. It should have been blue for a boy but Wullie did not notice. I sacrificed my hot-water bottle once again and he lay clutching it as he slept the clock round.

In a day or two he rose to the surface from time to time. I plied him with hot drinks, porridge, pudding, and kind words. 'You're nice,' he said drowsily, before drifting back to sleep. It gave a warm glow to my heart, better than a hot bottle. By now he had passed on his cough to me but I could cope with it, and at least we could bark away in unison, as if we were doing a duet.

When Wee Wullie was sitting up and beginning to look like a human being, the minister suddenly announced he would like to look in on the invalid.

'Hold on!' I cried in alarm. 'Wait till I warn him.'

I went coughing away to break the news to Wee

Wullie. 'The minister wants to come and see you.'

'O God!' exclaimed Wee Wullie and disappeared beneath the bedclothes.

Nothing would induce him to show his face. I heard H.J. coming and going without a word spoken. Then – there was more to the minister than met the eye – I heard a surprising sound. Music! H.J. had gone back to his study and picked up his fiddle. Now he was marching along the passage, into the kitchen, into the wee bedroom, playing a lively Scots reel. I followed behind to see what would happen. Presently a nose appeared above the covers. The next thing I saw was the minister perched on the bed, fiddling away for dear life with Wee Wullie sitting up and jiggling in time to the tune.

From that day on Wullie transferred his affections from me to the minister. I was still quite nice, but it was God who was the object of his complete devotion. When his cough finally left him – mine lingered on for ages – the small boy would lurk outside the study window listening for the strains of the violin, even if it was only H.J. practising his up-and-down scales. And Wee Wullie would hang around in a hope of 'running a message' for the minister. I sometimes invented jobs just to please him.

'Wullie, d'you think you could post this letter for the minister, please?'

'Oh ay, I will!' His face would light up and he was off like a shot to the pillar box.

Or I would say, 'The minister wonders if you could take the puppy for a run.'

'Oh ay! Come on, Bush!'

I had a kind of protective feeling towards Wullie, like a mother hen with a sickly chick. Being so small, he was fair game for bullies, and there were times when I had to restrain myself from going to his rescue, when I saw him being attacked in the school playground, lying squirming on the ground with a big laddie clutching him round the throat. Apart from the indignity of the 'Lady' of the Manse being involved in a brawl, I knew Wullie would have resented my interference. And often the wee warrior shook himself free, punched his adversary on the nose and strolled off the winner.

So I felt it wiser to leave him to fend for himself, but at least I could patch up his bleeding brow or black eye, as well as his jersey when it got torn. He was no longer afraid to come into the house. 'Is the meenister in?' he would ask eagerly.

'Yes, he's just taking off his Wellingtons. Maybe you could go and fetch them.'

'Oh ay, I will!' Anything to have a word with God.

So Wee Wullie and Oor Net were now part of the furnishings in the Manse and we all rubbed along as well as we could.

Oh! But it was a hard life as well as a hard frost. Many a time I could have given in and sat down for a good greet. I sometimes said to myself, 'I'll never last it out. No! I'll never!' I could scarcely remember a time when the sun shone and I was free to roam about the farm at home without a care in the world. I think I had reached my nadir on the day old Miss Calder came across with her yapping pug and said crossly, 'You'll have to come and help me. The bathroom thing's got stuck and it won't run away.'

'Ours is stuck, too.'

'Never mind! Come on! This is an emergency.'

His Reverence was always missing in an emergency. Right enough, he was out helping someone else who was in trouble, so it was left to me. It was a footering job which involved melting icicles after going out and breaking them off the outhouses where they hung in clusters. It did not do my cough much good; but at last the water in the bathroom cistern began to trickle.

'There!' said Miss Calder triumphantly, as if she had done it all by herself. 'See what can be done if you just try. You young folk . . .'

But I was away, biting my lips in case I let out one of Oor Net's words. She was waiting for me when I got back to the Manse.

'Oh miss! I've did a terrible thing.'

'Never mind, Nettie,' I said wearily. 'What is it?'

'Ye ken the meenister's dog collar?'

'Mercy! you haven't . . .'

'No, it was Bush. It fell on the flair an' the puppy got it. Damnation!'

Bush was sitting chewing it under the kitchen table. He looked happy enough so I just let him get on with it. It could have been worse. The ceiling hadn't fallen down yet.

'Keep going! Keep going!' I urged myself.

Then a day or two later a miracle happened. What was that strange sound? Drip-drip! Drip-drip! Could it be the thaw?

Yes! Mafeking was relieved!

But our troubles were not yet over. There is nothing more miserable than a cold thaw, and this was the coldest I had ever experienced. Because I was at my lowest ebb, physically, I shivered like a jelly as I tried to cope with this new emergency; for, from having too little water, we now had too much. It dripped and dropped from every eave, it trickled under the back door and the front door, it swamped the garden and ran like a river down the road. As fast as Nettie and I swept it out it came rushing in.

Water, water everywhere. But now at least we had a drop to drink.

The day came when H.J. could open the garage door and get out the Baby; but the greatest day of all was when we found the pump would work and we could light the kitchen range. Hot water at last!

We all pumped till we were breathless, then indulged in the luxury of hot baths. Even Nettie whom I persuaded to go up to the bathroom armed with a big towel and a sponge. 'Holy Moses! It's years since I've tooken a bath. I'll catch ma daith.' Instead of which, she came skipping downstairs as fresh as a daisy, saying, 'Thon's great, miss! Ye should have saw the waitter! Black as the deevil!'

Then one day the telephone rang. What a cheerful sound! Though there had been so much going on I had scarcely noticed its silence. Unlike the long winters in the farmhouse at home. The telephone was our lifeline, and when it broke down during a snow siege, we were completely cut off from the outside world. How we longed to hear Bella at the post office ringing us up to say, 'That's you back on the line. Are ye a' alive an' weel? D'ye ken the latest? The cat's kittled . . .'

As I went to pick up the receiver in the hall I keeked in the little mirror and saw a pale strained face. Could that peelly-wally creature be me? 'Put a smile on your face, wumman,' I told myself.

It was easy to smile when I heard who was speaking. Bella! I could have kissed the telephone.

'Hullo! Hullo! Overton Bush calling. Oh! it's you, lassie. Ay! They're tryin' to get in touch wi' ye. Ye've baith been cut off. Hasn't it been a beezer? An', d'ye ken what, auld Mrs Eliot's broken her leg again. Fell on the ice . . .'

My mother's voice came through. Oh! it was good to hear her. She wanted to speak to Sonny but he was out. I would get him to ring back when he came in. I wanted to speak to Jessie, though I knew she hated the telephone.

'Thon noisy beast!' she called it.

But, to my delight, she came.

'Hullo, Jessie.'

'HULLO!' she bawled, as if I was a million miles away, and so I was.

'How are you, Jessie?'

'Toots! I'm fine,' she said impatiently. 'How's yoursel'?'

'I'm fine, too,' said I, stifling my cough.

Then we were both stuck for words. To my surprise it was Jessie who filled the gap. 'I'm comin' doon to see ye.'

'WHAT?' I nearly fell over.

'They're gaun to gie me a hurl when the road's clear.'

'Oh Jessie! That's great! I'm dying to see you . . .'

'Toots!' she said and hung up.

The face in the mirror was now transformed. I pranced about in the hall and began to sing, 'Jesus loves me'!'

Well, somebody did!

A few days later Oor Net came into the kitchen with a strange expression on her face.

'Jings Geordie! D'ye ken what I've saw?'

'No, what?'

'A snawdrap in the gairden.'

I ran out to look. There it was, poking its nose bravely through the earth. I could have clapped my hands at such a cheerful sight, the promise of better things to come.

Like the snowdrop, we had come through.

6. The Gentry

There was only one mansion house – the Big Hoose – in the parish at home. The Laird lived there when he was not away in London engaged in his big business deals. He was a big man in every way and sat in the Laird's gallery on Sundays, gazing down at us lower mortals from his great height, like the Almighty. How did Sir J. M. Barrie, who was a frequent weekend guest and sat beside him like a wee gnome, comprehend a word he said?

I couldn't. He spoke with such an upper-class English accent; but I was not on speaking terms with the Almighty. Father was, but *he* could communicate on equal terms with a duke or a tramp and make them both laugh. The Laird had a strange guffaw. 'Haw-haw-HAW!' It was only Father who could tickle his funny bone.

The one time we understood the great man was when he came to inspect the village school and suggested to

Auld Baldy-Heid, the teacher, that we should be given a half holiday. We heard *that* all right and raised a cheer. But as for being on equal terms with the gentry, it never entered my head. They were moulded in a different pattern from me, not out of common clay.

There was not only one but several Big Hooses – even small castles – scattered around the Village district. Earthly mansions where the mighty lived in varying degrees of splendour, mainly retired people who, after busy and profitable lives in the outside world, had come to roost in their country retreats.

There was even a Sir and his Lady, as well as a Major and a Colonel who sometimes came to worship in the local kirk. And as there was no Laird's gallery in which to isolate them, and they could not rub shoulders with the common herd, they were shut into box-pews like mine, across the passage from me.

I sometimes keeked at them through my fingers during the prayers, and exchanged dignified bows when the kirk scaled, but I never vouchsafed a word. They were far above me.

Came the day when the minister and I were forced to visit them, for they had left cards, as well as gifts during the frost, and, mighty or not, they were part of my brother's flock. He took it all in his stride but I was petrified. O mercy me! Help!

Now that we were thawed out, His Reverence was raring to go, eager to visit everyone high and low. He considered it right and proper that I should accompany him on a first round of visits, so I tagged along. I liked the homely cottages best, though I lost my taste for tea after consuming so many cups of over-sweetened dark liquid.

'No! No more, thanks. That's plenty,' I would protest.

'Oh, go on, have another,' they would say, generously

ladling in a heaped teaspoonful of sugar. 'There! is that to your taste?'

'Oh yes, it's fine, thank you,' said I, bravely drinking it down. Heroic deeds are not always done on the battle-field.

My small talk grew smaller, but at least I could listen, and in any case I was overshadowed by His Reverence who went down a treat. Time and again the cottage wives would say to me in an aside. 'He's awful human, the minister.'

Yes! awful. You should hear him grumbling when he can't find his clean shirt in the morning.

Sometimes when I listened to them discussing him, I wondered if I was related to him at all. Was he just 'the minister', or had he ever been Sonny who ran barefoot about the farm and had his lugs clouted by Jessie?

But I had to admire him myself. I could see how his youth and openness appealed to his parishioners. He seldom mentioned biblical matters (at least not in my presence) but made contact with them on a wide range of other subjects. Farming, sport, local traditions, with the odd anecdote thrown in. If I was the listener, he was the talker, enjoying being the centre of attraction, and after all, that was his role as pastor. His flock put up with me as the minister's sister but it was Himself who scored the bull's-eye.

Part of his success was due to the fact that the previous preacher, though awful holy and awful upright, had also been awful strict, awful old, but not, I gathered, awful human. A rigid minister who had not moved with the times. No wonder Wee Wullie had been so terrified to come near the Manse.

The 'auld meenister' was spoken of with great respect and awe, not with much warmth. He had kept his place, aloof from his parishioners; but the new minister, full of energy and enthusiasm, was making a different place, side by side with his flock. There was nothing aloof about H.J.

Some of the older members raised their eyebrows when he appeared in plus fours and an open-necked shirt, but the young folk, so long neglected, rallied round him. As time went by he organized youth clubs, Scout camps and sporting events in which he competed himself. The auld meenister would have birled in his grave.

I never, of course, met the auld meenister. I would have been as frightened of him as Wee Wullie; but his sister – a proper Lady of the Manse – called unexpectedly one day. Veiled, gloved, button-booted, carrying a muff and wearing gold-rimmed pince-nez. As straight as a ramrod, the very essence of perjink propriety.

It was not one of my best days. I had baked a batch of scones which fell in the middle. (O Jessie! Where did I go wrong? Did I forget the self-raising powder?) 'Never mind! We can put plenty of jam on them and the minister'll maybe not notice,' I said to Nettie and went off to wash my hair.

It was standing up like a golliwog's when I came downstairs to dry it before the kitchen fire. The doorbell rang.

Oor Net went to answer it. She came back white-faced and shaken, tripping over her hen-toes. 'Michty God!'

'Nettie, will you please try not to . . .?'

She clapped her hand to her mouth. 'Canny help it! It just slipped oot. It's Her!'

'Her?'

'The auld meenister's sister! Holy Moses!'

Nettie had left her standing on the doorstep, and nothing would induce her to go back and usher the visitor in, so I was forced to do it myself. I gave my hair another rub, took a deep breath, and trailed away along the passage. The ex-Lady took one look at me and pursed her lips. She did not need to tell me what she was thinking.

I took her into the study. The minister, lucky devil, was out, but he had left traces behind him. I kicked the *Sporting Times* under the sofa and hastily picked up a golf ball. Then I cleared his fiddle off a chair and invited her to sit down. Tea! I rushed to the kitchen. No! Nettie flatly refused to bring it in. She would spread jam on the fallen scones and look out some cake, but she would not face the auld meenister's sister again. 'Michty God! No!'

The cake was stale, so was my conversation. I watched the visitor closely and hung on her every word. So *that* was what a real Lady of the Manse should be like. Never in a month of Sundays – years of Sundays – could I ever match up to someone as prim, proper and precise. How on earth, I wondered, had she and Ep got on? I never figured that one out.

The ex-Lady wanted to see everything upstairs and down. (Oor Net went and hid below the bed in the wee room off the kitchen.) Occasionally the visitor, looking around, would say 'Oh!' But what an 'Oh!' I had aged a hundred years by the time I showed her out.

Before tucking her gloved hands back into her muff, she looked down at the border beside the doorstep and said, 'Oh! Where's the candytuft I planted there?'

'Oh!' said I, but it was not her kind of 'Oh!' Doubtless I had howked up the candytuft thinking it was a weed. She went away shaking her head and I never saw her again. Neither of us was sorry.

After she left I went back to the kitchen with sagging shoulders. Then I sat down at the table and had another cup of tea with Oor Net. (She had fluff in her hair from below the bed. Oose!) What the dickens, I thought, defiantly putting my elbows on the table! I could never live up to *that*. Folk'll just have to take me as I am.

But I had lost my bravado by the time we went to visit the gentry.

Goodness! If I tried to put *them* in a book, who would believe me? I could scarcely believe in them myself. Someone surely must have invented them. Even watered down they seemed larger than life.

Not that they were all flamboyant. The Colonel, whom we visited first at The Sheiling, one of the smaller Big Hooses – a mere mansion – was leaning on a sundial in his garden wearing an old khaki uniform that was almost in tatters. He had a drooping ginger moustache which he chewed when asked a question. It saved him from talking. The Colonel did not speak much except in bursts like gunfire.

'Spring to it, fellow!' he would shout at me. I was used to being called 'Man-lassie', so I did not mind much; but it was a bit startling at first.

His wife was the talker and it was she who told us about the Colonel being imprisoned and tortured somewhere in the Middle East. He still had weals and wounds on his body. It was all to do with someone called Lawrence of Arabia.

She was very much the Colonel's lady, impressing us – and I was easily impressed – with tales of past grandeur, of glittering gatherings where she wore gorgeous gowns, of hobnobbing with royalty, of exotic palaces she had visited. She had found the perfect audience in me, but I could see H.J. growing a bit restless. I think he would sooner have talked to the Colonel, but *he* sat gazing into space, chewing his moustache.

When a sudden noise startled him, a door banging or a clock striking, he sprang to his feet and put up his fists. 'Now, now!' his wife would say soothingly and he would subside into silence.

As time went by I grew accustomed to his silences and sudden explosions. 'Spring to it, fellow!' He was really a gentle soul, and I would have liked to know him better and to ask about Lawrence of Arabia, but whenever I visited The Sheiling his wife commandeered me to listen to her tales of triumph. I think she quite liked me, though I was only a piece of blotting paper to her.

It was my brother who broke through the Colonel's barriers, and in future days I sometimes saw the pair of them leaning companionably against the sundial, deep in conversation. What were they discussing? Sport perhaps, for in his heyday the Colonel had been a runner and jumper, like H.J. I slunk past not to disturb them, and whenever I met the Colonel wandering about the lanes with that faraway look in his eyes, I was undecided whether to jouk into the side and ignore him, or to say, 'Good afternoon, Colonel.' Sometimes he recognized me and rapped out, 'Hullo fellow!' to which I replied, 'Hullo, sir!'

He could sometimes be seen hanging about outside the kirk on Sundays. He never came in. The church bells and the organ startled him. Perhaps he was waiting for his lady wife who came to worship now and again wearing one of her feathery hats. Or maybe he was hoping for a word with H.J. It was strange how soon we came to accept him as normal.

But what is normal?

Maybe the gentry thought we, my brother and I, were an odd pair. Certainly *I* felt odd the first day we were bidden to lunch at the knight's table. 'About one-thirty,' which seemed late to me. I was starving by then and I could hear the minister's tummy rumbling by the time we were seated at the polished dining-room table. But in the event I scarcely ate a bite or said a word; it was all so strange and unlikely.

Fancy the Lady, our hostess, wearing a straw hat with a veil in her own house and not knowing what we were going to eat! 'Ah! kidneys!' she said in a surprised and delighted voice when a serving-maid, who addressed her as 'M'lady' offered them to her in a silver chafing dish. She did not know her maids' names, I learnt later, nor the way to the kitchen, I suspected. I would have been mentally if not physically dashing backwards and forwards a dozen times to see if Oor Net had dished the cauliflower or burned the potatoes. Likely as not, I would have peeled the tatties myself, but Lady Victoria could not even do her own hair. Perhaps that was why she was wearing a hat, or was it the done thing at upper-class lunch parties?

Sir Joseph was a gentleman. A gentle man in every way; good-looking, gallant, gracious. He had certainly come out of the topmost drawer. He spoke like the Laird at home and treated me as if *I* was royalty, though I felt I ought to bob a curtsey to *him*.

The only other member of the party was a daughter whom they called Darling. Her real name, I discovered, was Aileen; a pale languid youngish lady who seemed to find a soup spoon too heavy to handle. She was like someone in a poem.

> I met a lady in the meads
> Full beautiful, a faery's child.
> Her hair was long, her foot was light,
> And her eyes were wild.

Aileen's eyes were not wild but empty, I thought, as if there was nothing much in life for her except her parents' devotion. She gave me sidelong glances now and then as she nibbled at her food, drooping over her plate like a wilting lily. ('Shouthers back!' Jessie would have shouted at her.) She was delicate, her parents told me. It was a full-time job, dawdling from one thing to another. A glass of sherry midmorning, a little walk with her spaniel, a siesta, a trail round the garden to pick some flowers, dress for dinner and the day was done.

I felt over sturdy in comparison; yet when I caught one of her glances, I thought, 'Maybe there's more in you, Darling, than meets the eye.'

(How was I to guess we would become such firm friends and remain so till the day she died, many years later?)

What white hands they all had, I noticed! I made mine into fists and hid them in my lap. The ladies, of course, never sullied theirs; but Sir Joseph, with his long sensitive fingers, had been an eminent surgeon in his day, and had cut up more interesting meat than the silverside he was dissecting so neatly. Even royal flesh, I was told.

At the start of the meal my brother cleared his throat. He was anxious to get at the food, I knew, but there was the tricky problem of grace. To pray or not to pray. We observed the old proprieties at the Manse even if only feasting off toasted cheese, and had always gabbled a grace at the farmhouse at home. 'Bless this food – mumble-mumble – Amen!' But with Sir Joseph already munching his roll and his Lady swallowing her first spoonful of soup, the minister was in a quandary. So he just closed his eyes and did his own private mumbling before picking up his spoon and getting on with it.

I wished they would all get on with it and not bother about me. 'Ignore me! I'm not here! I'm quite content just watching and listening.' But breeding will out. Sir Joseph engaged me in conversation about the weather. Hadn't it been severe? 'Oh, very severe!' And how did I like living in the country? 'Fine!' (I had never lived anywhere else but in the country.) Lady Victoria asked me if I hunted much. 'No, not much!' Darling attempted to pass me the cream jug before a maid took it out of her frail hand.

I felt as if I had been wafted away to another world and, when I got back to the Manse kitchen, I had to eat some bread and cheese to settle my floating stomach.

'Jings Geordie!' exclaimed Nettie. 'Did they no' gie ye naethin' to eat?'

It took a long time for my first blurred impressions to sharpen, but gradually I grew to like the gentry, to be less tongue-tied in their presence, and to recognize that though their hands were whiter than mine, we were not all that different under the skin.

From the start I got on like a house on fire with the Major, though he had the reputation of being crusty. He looked a choleric wee man, tubby with waxed moustaches, the type who might rap out orders or be given to sudden outbursts of rage. But he was as meek as milk with me. Perhaps because of the pianola.

'That awful instrument!' his wife called it, chiding the Major because of his partiality for playing it.

I was fascinated by the pianola. I had never seen one before, and was content to sit for ages beside the Major on a long piano stool in the drawing room while invisible hands played tinkly tunes on the keyboard, and the magic rolls went winding their way round and round.

The 'Blue Danube' was the Major's favourite. Mine, too, for I had never heard it played all the way through without hiccuping in the middle, as it did on our old gramophone at home. The Major could make it go fast or slow, loud or soft. I thought he was a better player than Paderewski.

He was like a little boy with a toy. 'Shall we go in and play some music?' he would say to me out of the corner of his mouth, while the others were finishing their afternoon tea on the lawn.

'Oh yes, please!'

Sometimes he let me have a turn at working the pianola, but his renderings were better than mine; and I knew how much he enjoyed working it, so I just sat back and left it to him. There was no need for conversation. The pianola spoke for us both.

The Major and his family lived at The Heugh. It was the largest of the mansion houses in the district; a small castle, with turrets and towers, a gazebo and greenhouses in the terraced gardens, and grounds that included a tennis court and a game called clock golf. We were often bidden there in the summer when The Heugh was filled with visitors. Mainly to tennis parties.

My problem was what to wear. It was all right for H.J. who had proper whites from his college days; flannels, shoes, socks, shirts, and the right racquet. I could turn *him* out looking the part, but how was I to dress? The best I could muster was a skirt and blouse, and a shabby pair of sandshoes. I tried to keep on the sidelines with a middle-aged woman called Dolly, who did not look a bit like a doll. A poor relation who acted as a kind of lady-in-waiting for the Major's wife, fetching and carrying, always grateful when anyone spoke to her, but never pushing herself forward.

Sometimes *I* got pushed forward to make up a foursome. I was not a bad player when given a chance, and once in a fit of exasperation I got so carried away with the game that I called my partner, an etiolated young man from London, a silly sumph. It was tantamount to hitting him over the head with my racquet, but luckily he had no notion what I meant, and just grinned feebly at me, then lisped, 'Oh! I thay!'

If the Major was besotted with his pianola his wife was

obsessed with her flower garden. God wot!

She was an imposing lady, plump and motherly, and it was out of kindness, I am sure, that she took me round the garden one summer day and introduced me to every single blossom. Mrs Major carried a pair of shears and snipped bits off here and there, while I trailed behind her, not really recognizing anything except the odd pansy or poppy and saying, 'Oh yes! lovely!' to everything. She knew them all by their rude Latin names. Not only that, I had to linger at each flowerbed while she gave me a blow-by-blow account of their antecedents, how she had transplanted them from here to there, what kind of soil they preferred, and promised me cuttings. Oh jings! I was sure to kill them off.

Now and again I made an intelligent observation. 'There's a nice little thing. What's that?' indicating a wee blue flower.

'A weed,' said Mrs Major, yanking it out pitilessly. Poor thing! It was not on the social register, not to be classed with the superior Latin blooms, though it looked every bit as pretty.

Suddenly I did recognize something I knew. 'Oh look!' I cried. Leckie, the Tattie-Bogle, leaning on a spade. Obviously he spread his favours around.

'Hullo!' I said, relieved to see something human, even if it was only him.

He touched his forelock, not to me but to Mrs Major, who just gave him an offhand nod and said, 'I don't like the look of that herbaceous border, Leckie.'

'No, ma'am,' said he, with another touch to his cap, and shuffled off towards the compost heap.

Mrs Major sighed and gazed around the garden. 'If only you had seen it last week! It was a blaze of colour.'

*

That was all away in the future. Forget the gentry. They were nothing compared with the fact that Jessie's visit was looming near.

7. Onward Christian Soldiers

Oor Net was up to High Doh.

So was I. If royalty had been expected we could not have made more thorough preparations. Nettie had washed the front doorstep twice and gone down on her hunkers to polish the waxcloth even in the darkest passage leading to the kitchen. She had also scrubbed out her mouth to make sure she didn't let a 'Damnation' escape, and was practising 'Deary me!' instead. It was the minister's parents she was worrying about, but I was thinking of Jessie.

I had told Nettie something about her and given her a warning. 'She's awful nice, Jessie, but a wee bit sharp-tongued. You mustn't mind what she says.'

'Och, deary me, I'm easy. I'll no' mind *her*. Is the meenister's mother awfu' perjink?' (She was *my* mother, too, though Oor Net didn't seem to realize it.) 'Wad she

76

notice a hole in ma heel?'

'No, *she*'s easy. But Jessie might. You'd better darn in.'

'Holy Moses!' groaned Nettie and went off in search of a darning needle.

The fires were burning cheerfully and appetizing smells coming from the kitchen. I was no great shakes as a cook but I had baked a passable apple pie, cooked a pot roast, a panful of stovies and made lentil soup with a hambone. Plain fare, but wholesome and to Jessie's taste. It was her I was thinking of all the time, though try as I would to see her face, I had forgotten what she looked like.

But wait till she came. I would recognize her then. It was too good to be true.

I hung about at the door waiting for a first sight of Father's rattletrap. Then I heard a distressed call from the kitchen. 'Michty God! The stovies have went an' stuck to the pan.'

'Shake them, Nettie! Shake them! They're coming!'

Father was honking his horn and the motor juddering to a standstill. Even when the engine was turned off, it always continued to shake and rattle before it settled down. Mother was sitting in front wearing a blue motoring veil over her hat. An upright figure was sitting in the back.

Jessie! How could I have forgotten what she looked like? She was just the same, wearing her good costume, a black hat, and a pair of knitted gloves. She held a small parcel in her hands.

When she got out of the car I forgot myself, ran forward, grabbed her round the neck and pressed a kiss on her cheek.

'Away!' she said, fending me off as if she had been stung by a wasp, and handed me the parcel. It contained treacle toffee (trykle taffy, she called it) as I discovered later. She thought I looked peaky.

'No, I'm fine,' I protested, and grew finer every minute she was there.

It was nice seeing Mother and Father, though they naturally were more interested in Sonny and spent a great deal of time with him in the study. That suited me fine, for I could have Jessie to myself. We had a fly cup of tea in the kitchen, with Nettie standing gawping on one leg.

'Tell me everything, Jessie. Everything!'

'What aboot?'

'How's Jock?'

'Och! He's fine. Except for a sair thoomb.'

'Oh! What happened?'

'Clipped it wi' the shears, but daursay he'll survive. Watch the tatties, Nettie!'

In five minutes she had taken command. How I wished she could stay for ever and ever. After appraising Oor Net, and when she was safely out of earshot in the back kitchen, Jessie admitted, 'I've seen worse. Ye're no' bein' ower saft wi' her?'

'No, I'm very firm,' I lied.

She had brought her knitting with her, a long black stocking. It was great to hear the click of her needles, and her tongue, biting as ever.

'Watch oot, wumman!' she said sharply to Nettie. 'Ye'll coup that pan.'

She refused to have her meal in the dining room with the rest of us. 'No! I'll cairry in the plates. Have ye heated them, Nettie?'

'Ay, I have.'

Not a wrong word passed Oor Net's lips. She bobbed a curtsey to my mother, and was greatly taken by Father who opened the dining-room door for her.

'*She*'s a lady, the meenister's mother,' she whispered

78

to me later. Obviously I wasn't, but I didn't care. I was a
lassie again, sitting at Jessie's knee.

I took her all over the house and showed her everything. 'My!' she said at intervals. I think she felt sorry for
me having to cope with such a rambling domain. My
own room was the untidiest. There had been no time to
redd it up, so there were books spilling on the floor and a
clutter of notebooks and pencils on the bed.

'I see ye've no' improved,' she remarked.

'No, I've not,' I said guiltily.

'A'weel!' sighed Jessie as if I was past hope. 'I see ye're
still scribblin'!'

'Yes, when I get the chance.'

Watch out, Jessie, I thought! Maybe I'll write about
you some day.

I couldn't get over the fact that she was here. Somehow
the Manse had become a home for the first time, with her
in the kitchen asking for a loan of Nettie's apron. 'I think
I'll just thraw up a scone for the tea.'

Wee Wullie was keeking round the back door, not sure
whether to come in or to go away.

'Come in if ye're comin' in,' said Jessie. 'Sit doon an'
keep quiet.'

I had to go off and talk to my parents. They wanted to
hear all about the gentry. 'Oh, *them!*' Mother gave me
some sage advice about returning their hospitality, but I
hardly listened.

When I got back to the kitchen, Wee Wullie was sitting
on a stool at Jessie's knee, the way I used to sit in the byre
when she was milking the kye, and she was telling him a
story. The one about the moudiwart, the wee mole who
lived under the ground. Wee Wullie was hanging on
every word, and so was Oor Net, standing sucking her
thumb, completely absorbed. The scones were cooling
on a wire tray on the table, and the kettle was boiling.

Jessie brought the story to an end. I could have echoed the familiar words myself.

'An the wee moudiwart took oot his handkie, dichted his een, an' never grat anither tear for the rest o' his life.'

'Ah-hh!' sighed Wee Wullie and Oor Net in unison, disappointed that the story was over but satisfied with its happy ending.

'That's it!' said Jessie, rising to her feet. 'Set oot the tea, Nettie.'

When I saw the motor disappearing, I felt so homesick I had to dicht ma een, like the wee moudiwart to stop me from bubbling. I might have given in and gone to my room had not Oor Net reverted to normal and cried, 'Damnation! I've went an' broke the teapot stroup. It's a mercy Jessie didny see me.'

'Never mind. We've got another, I think, on the top shelf. Bring it down. Oh, and by the way, Jessie thought you were doing fine.'

Nettie blushed bright pink with pleasure as she raxed down the teapot. It nearly slipped out of her hands as she repeated what she had already told me. 'The meenister's mother's a real lady, an' so's his faither. I mean he's a gent.'

I had noticed Father giving her some money out of his pocket before he left, and wished he had slipped something into my hand, too. Nobody thought of giving me a salary, however small, or making me an allowance, and I was often hard-pressed to pay for personal items. It was a tight enough squeeze, trying to stretch the housekeeping budget.

But what did it matter? It was only money. I felt rich because of something Jessie said when we parted.

'Ye'll get by, lassie. I've got faith in ye.'

And then I knew for sure by the way she looked at me, Jessie was fond of me. It was better than money.

★

Now that I had been blooded by making my visitations with the minister, I had hoped for a respite. But no! My parish duties were only beginning. Mrs Sturrock, the chief elder's wife, made this abundantly clear when she called one afternoon while I was giving Bush a long overdue bath; and a right mess he made of her good skirt when he frisked around her sturdy ankles.

'Down, doggy, down!' said Mrs Sturrock, trying not to sound too severe to the Manse puppy, though I could see she was dying to kick him.

I shut Bush in the back kitchen and solaced her with tea and dropscones while she reeled off a long list of duties expected of me. I would go round with a collecting book, attend the Women's Guild meetings, take my turn at doing the flowers on Sunday, visit old Mrs Somebody who was bedridden (I had already visited her but, of course, I would go again), take over the Brownies, and could I sing in the Choir? No! I couldn't! Well, could I take a Sunday-school class?

'Oh please, Mrs Sturrock, shut up and go away!' I kept urging her silently. As the list grew longer, so did my face, but Mrs Sturrock looked increasingly pleased with herself.

'You'll soon find plenty to do,' she assured me as we parted at the door.

'You're telling me!' I said under my breath as I shut her out.

I went to the Women's Guild meeting in the church hall, the youngest member there, though goodness knows I was growing older every minute. They were about to hold a knitting competition when I arrived. Cast on a sock and see how much – and how evenly – you could knit in half an hour. Meanwhile, Mrs Sturrock would read to us from an improving book about someone called Mary Slessor.

'*You* don't need to do it,' Mrs Sturrock said to me kindly. But I did and won. If it had been sewing I would have been sunk. (Even today when I cast on a sock, I think of Mary Slessor and her noble deeds.)

It was my first triumph. The women looked at me with some respect and unanimously elevated me to the chair. I would have to take over as President of the Women's Guild, I was told. It was the done thing for the Lady of the Manse to hold that high office.

Oh Lord, help me! There was more to it than knitting socks. I would have to begin and end the meetings with prayer; even go to the General Assembly in Edinburgh. Well, Jessie had faith in me so there was nothing else for it but to try.

I got on fine with the Brownies. I was supposed to give them a lesson in tying knots, but I hadn't practised and got tied in knots myself. So I suggested a game of Puss-in-the-corner instead. They liked that better and seemed surprised that I could run with such speed from one corner of the hall to another, hissing 'Puss-puss'. They had expected me to stand still and blow my whistle, but it was great to kick up my heels and feel the blood coursing through my veins.

'She's not bad,' I heard one small Brownie whisper to another. I took it as a great compliment.

Mrs Sturrock was right. I found plenty to do.

I went round with a collecting book in aid of the Schemes of the Church. What on earth was the church scheming about, I wondered, as I walked the long miles from one habitation to another? There was a wee book with all the names in it of folk who had previously contributed. A sixpence here, a shilling there. It all added up.

'And how's the minister?'

'Oh, he's fine!'

A visit from *him* would have set them up for the day, but I was the next best thing. I tried to confine my calls to doorstep encounters, but no! I must come in. A chair was dusted for me to sit on, and the kettle boiled. 'More tea?' 'Oh no, thank you! I couldn't drink another drop.'

It was difficult to know how and when to escape without causing offence. They all wanted to know about His Reverence and how he was liking his new parish. 'Oh, he loves it!' I told them, laying it on thick. But it was true, and they took it as a personal compliment.

I lingered longer with the isolated ones and was pleased to find some of them interested in me, not just the minister.

'You'll come back?'

'Oh yes, I will, Mrs Greig. Take care of that leg.'

Sometimes when I saw them fumbling in their purses and counting out the coins, I worried about whether they could afford the sixpences and shillings. 'You don't *need* to give,' I would say. (Not much of a saleswoman for the Church's schemes.) But they insisted. If their name was in the book they must keep up the tradition. Some even increased their contributions. 'Because we like the new minister.'

Good for H.J.!

And good for me. Since there was no one else to do it, I gave myself a pat on the back now and then. Sometimes I wondered if I would ever have a life of my own again. I must hang on to my own identity, whatever it was, and not just be 'the minister's sister'. Find time, I told myself, to get on with your writing. Time!

I sometimes thought out stories as I walked about on my duties, but this was dangerous, for I would go off into a dwam and brush past parishioners, forgetting to say, 'Good afternoon, Mrs Moffat. Has Jenny got over her sore throat?'

Once I bumped into the minister and gave him a vague greeeting, then, recognizing him: 'Oh hullo! It's only you!'

There was no denying H.J. was making a real impact. I heard his praises sung on all sides and felt pleased for his sake. His sermons were good. More lively, they said – and shorter – than the auld meenister's. My problem was to avoid falling asleep in the house of God. It was my only chance of sitting still for any length of time, but it was not only God who was watching. Mrs Sturrock and the rest of the congregation had their eagle eyes on me. So I dug the nails of one hand into the palm of the other to keep myself alert and gazed at the pulpit with a fixed expression on my face. Pious, I hoped.

Though he was on such intimate terms with the Almighty and a hero to his parishioners, H.J. was a handless creature when it came to practical matters. Even making tea for himself. On rare occasions when I had been delayed at a meeting I hurried home dreading to smell burnt toast and hear the minister's aggrieved greeting. 'Where have you been? And where's Nettie? I had to get my own tea!'

He would sit down in a huff while I repaired the damage and feel badly done by for the rest of the day.

True enough, Oor Net was not always at her post when she should have been, but how could I blame her, for she was only a young lassie?

Sometimes she sneaked across to the school where she had so recently been a pupil, and joined a group of big girls in the playground, jumping in a line through a skipping-rope. I could hear her happily shouting 'Holy Moses!' and hadn't the heart to call her back to peel the potatoes. I would fain have joined in the line myself.

It was a case of Nettie putting up with me and I with her, though there were times when I felt a trifle swamped by the Hogg family. ('Going the whole Hogg,' the minister called it, with an unusual flash of wit.) In a family crisis, and there were many, Oor Net would bring the puking baby with her. He would lie in the bed in the little room off the kitchen, kicking up his bare legs. Or more often just kicking up a row.

'Can't you keep that baby quiet?' the minister, disturbed in his sermon, would shout to me from the study. And I would have to leave whatever I was doing, lift up Henry John and shoogle him in my arms. 'Deedle-deedle-dumpling, my son John, went to bed with his britches on.'

I felt the minister ought to have dandled his own namesake but his mind was on higher things. Wee Wullie, of course, was a constant caller, so sometimes I handed the baby over to him while I got on with my chores. Chores! There was never an end to them. Nor an end to the visitors who came to the front and back doors.

The only time I felt I was myself was when I could call in briefly at old Sarah's sweetie shop and converse with her in the broad dialect. No need to be perjink. She treated me like a human being, not the minister's sister, and used old sayings familiar to me through Jessie and Jock-the-herd. 'It tak's a stoot hert to a stey brae!' I knew what that meant all right. (A stout heart to a steep hill.) Old Sarah brought a touch of reality into my muddled life, though I always felt more homesick for the farmhouse and the hills of home when I left her to hurry back to the Manse.

I was always in a hurry, walking as briskly as I could without breaking into an undignified trot. 'Oh! hullo, Mrs Scott.' 'Yes, thank you, the minister's fine.' 'Good evening, Mr – er – whatever-your-name-is . . .' If there was no one in sight, I did run, almost gallop.

My only other form of release was when I occasionally

took the puppy for a run in the gloaming. Well, *he* ran and I walked as quickly as I could without actually scampering after him. If Wee Wullie had not been able to take him out and the minister was too occupied with his own ploys, I could not resist the puppy's pleadings when he kept jumping up on me, begging to be let out of prison. I knew the feeling.

'Right-o, then! Come on, Bush!' I would say, picking up his lead and shoving a tammy on my head. 'But it'll have to be quick.'

There were fewer folk about at the darkening of the day, and I could sometimes let him off his lead so that he could frisk ahead of me with countless detours and snuffings in the hedgerows. I could not go up the Loaning for old Miss Calder would be sure to collar me, and Bush would fight with her yapping pug. So I usually ran along the lane leading to the Big Hooses where there was not much traffic. If I encountered the Colonel I would just say, 'Good evening, sir' and slink past. 'Come on, Bush! Quick march!'

One evening the puppy ran on ahead of me and I heard him barking excitedly. Had he raised a hedgehog, perhaps, or was he chasing after a rabbit? Then I saw another dog, a spaniel, and a faint figure in the half-light, trying to disentangle herself from the lead that had wound itself round her legs. I hurried forward to help her. 'Down, Bush!'

'Oh, it's you,' she said, straightening herself out. Then I recognized her, the pale delicate daughter from one of the Big Hooses. Darling, whose real name was Aileen, and whose father was a Sir.

'Are you out for a walk?' she asked in her low soft voice.

'More like a run,' I said, firmly attaching Bush to his lead. 'I'll have to go. I'm in a hurry.' (How often I was to say the same words to her in our future meetings!)

She turned and walked beside me and I had to slow my pace to match hers. 'What are you hurrying back for?' she wanted to know.

'To make the minister's supper.'

'Oh!' This was a feat beyond her comprehension. 'What is it to be?'

'Toad-in-the-hole,' I told her, but I could see she had no conception of how toads got into holes. Then, to be polite, I asked, 'Where are you going?'

'Just taking Jasper for a little walk before dinner.'

Someone meantime would be cooking the dinner, setting the silver on the table, and Aileen would have no idea what the first, second or third courses were to be. And no washing-up afterwards.

She seemed loth to part when we came within sight of the Manse. 'You must be very busy,' she remarked, giving me one of her sidelong glances.

'Och well!' I said, 'there's always plenty to do.' Then I found myself saying, 'What about you?' before I remembered that being delicate was a full-time job.

'Well . . .' She gave a self-conscious cough. 'I try to do a bit of writing.'

I nearly shouted 'Holy Moses!' It was the first time I had met another human being with the same interests. 'I write a bit, too,' I confessed.

And then the floodgates opened.

We began to gabble, one to the other, we had so much to say. Well! I gabbled and Aileen spoke faster than I thought she could, growing more animated every minute, for she, too, was out on a limb with no one to talk to about her writing. But a different limb from mine. She had a writing room all to herself,. and a maid who dusted her pencils every morning (I once saw her doing it) before straightening them out into neat rows on her desk.

She had all day in which to write, but she got tired and needed inspiration. Yes! She'd had something published, a piece in a prestigious paper called *Punch*, a first success. But they had refused everything she subsequently sent. She was now vaguely collecting material for a book on Nell Gwyn, but it was very tedious and she would sooner do some shorter stuff, only she didn't know anything about markets.

'I'll lend you my *Writers' and Artists' Year Book*,' I offered. A treasure I had lately acquired. 'I must run.'

'But I'll see you again?'

'Oh yes!'

It was the first of many hurried meetings and before long we were on first-name terms, even though we were such different peas from different pods. Sir Joseph and his Lady approved of the friendship and said I was good for Darling, who certainly looked less languid after our encounters. It was good for me, too, though I never had time to look languid. We inspired each other to try different markets and discussed every dot and comma we had written. But oh dear! I was always in a hurry. 'I *must* rush!'

Aileen turned and walked away with a brisker step, and I ran hell-for-leather back to the Manse to cope with the toad-in-the-hole.

8. Kist O' Whustles

'Give me an A,' said the minister, tuning his fiddle.

Yes! I could do that. I thumped it out on the old drawing-room piano.

'Are you sure that's an A?' asked H.J. doubtfully.

'It's the best I can do. The piano needs tuning.'

So did I.

It was not fair to blame the piano for being timmer. (Another of Jessie's words: timmer meaning tuneless.) Even on a perfect grand, my A's never sounded right. That went for my other notes as well.

In truth, I was not a natural musician, and would sooner have played the Major's pianola. Perhaps the blame could be traced back to Miss Todd, the piano teacher, who cycled out from Jedburgh once a week to give me lessons at the farmhouse. After her exertions she was in no mood for teaching, but sat back chatting to my mother, drinking tea and eating scones, only occasionally turning her attention to me.

'*Thumb*-one-two-three, dear! *Thumb*-one-two-three!' she would say, stirring her tea and only half listening to my mistakes. Even today when faced with a sheet of music I think '*Thumb*-one-two-three,' and see Miss Todd helping herself to another scone.

We worked from a book called *Hemy's Tutor for the Pianoforte* which included such tuneful gems as 'Le Carnaval de Venise' (six-eight time, count six quavers in a bar), 'Home to our Mountains', and 'Gaily the Troubadour'.

Eventually I could thump out 'Für Elise', 'The Harmonious Blacksmith' (a misnomer) and a dreadful dirge called 'Handel's Largo'. And when we had visitors for the evening and were called upon to show off our accomplishments, if I could not escape in time I was forced to play 'The Bluebells of Scotland'. With variations! But I hated 'performing'.

I was quite good at inventing little tunes – *Thumb*-one-two-three – that were no worse in my opinion than Handel's dreary Largo. But now, in my new role as Lady of the Manse, I had no time for such flights of fancy, apart from tinkling out 'Here We Go Round the Mulberry Bush' for the Brownies who never noticed my discords, or washing a sailor's shirt while dusting the discordant piano.

This was different.

The minister had agreed to play the fiddle at a social gathering to be held in the church hall, and I was to accompany him. Not only to the social but on the piano. Help! H.J. liked showing off his prowess in public. He had something to show. I hadn't.

'Couldn't you get somebody else?' I pleaded with him.

'No; you'll do fine.'

We had no metronome so he just thumped his feet on the carpet. '*Thumb*-one-two-three!'

The music placed in front of me bore no resemblance whatsoever to that H.J. had set up on the music stand, so while he was playing one tune I was playing another which was no tune at all, only a series of disconnected chords which were supposed to merge into a melodious duet. Only, of course, if we kept together! It was not so much a case of accompanying my brother as chasing after him.

'Just you go on by yourself,' I said to him. 'I'll catch up!'

Sometimes in a fit of bravado I overtook him. We were lucky, indeed, if we ended in a dead heat. It was murder.

Bush came and sat under the piano for a while, then lifted up his head and howled like a soul in torment. H.J. practically kicked him downstairs. I wished he would do the same to me; but I had to stick it out, saved only by the doorbell ringing at intervals. Then I would abandon the keyboard and slide down the bannisters to answer it.

'Hurry back,' said the minister, plucking impatiently at his strings, but I took my time and climbed back upstairs at a snail's pace.

It was not easy to fit in a practice and be at H.J.'s beck and call whenever he wanted to 'go over the music'. Sometimes I had to sit at the piano up to the elbows in flour after being called away from humbler tasks. The photograph of Jedburgh Abbey on the piano shivered and shook. How I longed to be there instead of here.

We had to have several pieces ready in case we got an encore. 'O please! No!' I prayed to the Lord.

We got *two* encores. It wasn't fair.

The parishioners were so taken on at having a fiddling minister that they clapped like mad and thumped their feet on the floor. 'Encore! Encore!' As for me, the thing to do, I discovered, was to play as softly as I could, not to be obtrusive and let H.J. get on with it. He took all the bows and the praise and I didn't mind a bit.

'Isn't the minister a great player?' the folk said to me afterwards.

'Yes, isn't he!' I agreed, thinking, thank goodness it's over.

But it wasn't. It was only the beginning.

Flushed with triumph, the minister decided to get up a concert party. There was a dearth of entertainment in the district, though I hadn't noticed it. Of course, H.J. was used to the capital city of Edinburgh where everything happened. I thought the Village teemed with activity compared with the quiet life I had led in the remote farmhouse at home, and would have welcomed a night off and a good read.

Not the energetic minister who liked to have his diary full to overflowing, though he groaned and grumbled about it. 'Gracious! I see I've got to go out again tonight. Why did I agree to speak at that meeting at Chirnside?' Or somewhere.

'Because you're daft!' I muttered under my breath. 'And because you enjoy being in the public eye.'

He did.

But it was not only his own talent he wanted to show off. There were others in the parish who ought to be encouraged to 'do things'. If he banded them together they would have the makings of a good concert party. A concert party, anyway.

There was Bob Somebody from the church choir who could sing high and Jim Somebody who sang low. And a stout lady who was a contralto if anything. Mrs Stout had a passable voice, a large chest but a very small repertoire, consisting mainly of 'When We Go Down the

Vale, Lads' and 'Hail Caledonia'. There was a wee man who gave big licks to 'The Cottar's Saturday Night'. And there was His Reverence on the fiddle. He had quite a passable voice, too, and sometimes sang a solo. 'On the Road to Mandalay'.

What more could anyone want?

The awful thing was I had to play for the lot.

We held some fearful rehearsals in the Manse, and I had to provide tea and sandwiches for the cast as well as struggle with 'Trumpeter, what are you sounding now?' Bush got shut in the back kitchen where I would willingly have joined him, and I fell far behind with darning the minister's socks. But this was culture and took precedence over all else.

I hope never to hear 'Hail Caledonia' again or listen to that Scottish Medley which His Reverence got up as a grand finale. *Thumb*-one-two-three! Thump-thump! Jim Somebody sometimes lost his voice through sheer terror and had to be revived with tumblers of water. I kept a jug on the piano just in case.

'I'll never manage,' he kept saying, mopping his fevered brow, but the minister steeled him by quoting Bruce and the spider. Try, try, try again!

It is all a blur to me now. It happened gradually over our first year at the Village, not everything at once. But at long last we were ready to launch ourselves on the waiting world. The first concert was even announced from the pulpit, and posters put up. They left my name off which was kind of them.

I cannot recall that first performance, only a *mélange* of concerts held in dimly-lit halls all over the county (for our fame spread and we were in great demand in all the neighbouring parishes), of travelling over icy roads in the Baby Austin, with a van containing the rest of the cast following behind us, of draughty stages and untuned pianos, of praying in vain there would not be a *third* encore, and of the 'wee teas' served up to us afterwards by the grateful organizers. It was all awful.

By the end of the concert the performers were so wound up they would willingly have given a *fourth* encore if encouraged. But I knew how to play the National Anthem, if nothing else, so I hastened to thump it out the moment the grand finale came to a close, causing everyone to stand loyally to attention. I had to stand, too, while playing it. It was the done thing in those days.

As for sitting, I was provided with a strange assortment of creaky chairs and stools at the pianos, some far too high, others far too low. Once one of the chair legs gave way and I collapsed on the stage. It was the only time I got a round of applause, but H.J. was cross, for he was busy pizzicatoing at the time and it put him off the stot.

I have recollections of shivering most of the time, not just with nerves but goose pimples. The halls were so chilly and the stages so draughty I often longed for a hot-water bottle on my lap and woolly gloves to warm my icy fingers. Sometimes the piano was on the stage, sometimes down below where the lighting was so dim I could scarcely see the keyboard let alone the notes on the music sheets. Indeed, the minister was lucky if he got an A when he was tuning up.

The audience could sit huddled in their coats, but the performers had to be dressed up to some degree. The men attired themselves in their Sunday suits, and the ladies (there were only two of us) were toshed up in 'good frocks', the nearest we had to evening dress.

This posed a problem to me and I was in a quandary till I unearthed some leftover curtain material. Dark blue with faint pink squiggles on it. It hung on every window in the Manse, but there was enough for me to make a straight up-and-down dress. No sleeves. I didn't know how to sew them in. And as I was a skinnymalink with matchstick arms, it was little wonder I often had the shivers.

But who would look at me when they could gaze on Mrs Stout in all her glory?

I often wished I could warm my hands on *her*. She was the nearest thing to a hot-bottle, so buxom she seemed to be bursting at every seam. Mrs Stout had not only one but three good frocks, all brightly coloured and too tight. Her favourite was the scarlet one with artificial flowers at her ample bosom. From the corner of my eye I could see them wobbling as she hit the high notes while hailing Caledonia.

The green one was too short, so she spent a great deal of time on stage tugging it down. The third was yellow with roundabout stripes which made her look like a bumblebee. But she had no sting, and was an amiable body, popular with audiences who encored her time and again. She not only bowed to them but curtseyed at the end, with unfortunate results when she was wearing her green. Her *directoire* knickers were known the length and breadth of the country.

The minister's diary grew fuller. He thrived on it, but oh! how I longed for a peaceful evening at home. ('Yes, thank you, Mrs Sturrock. I'm finding plenty to do.') Nothing, I thought, could be worse than those awful concert parties.

I was wrong.

Miss Steele, the organist, who was a nice woman but only human, took ill. Who was to fill in while she was away in hospital?

Oh no! Not me! Please, not that!

'Yes! There's nobody else,' said the minister firmly.

H.J. was great at sorting things out.

I had never played the organ before and I hope I never will again, after those nightmarish Sundays while Miss Steele was getting something extracted from her insides. How willingly I would have changed places with her! 'Take all my organs,' I pleaded with the Almighty. 'Only don't make me play the church one.'

He never listened, of course; and after that I lost all pity for Job. What were his sufferings compared with mine?

It was an American organ – a kist o' whustles – which had to be pedalled by foot. It was good exercise, which was the last thing I needed, and who would want to ride a bicycle in full view of the congregation instead of snoozing in the privacy of a box-pew?

It was hopeless trying to get to grips with *Vox Humana* and all the other stops which had to be pulled out and pushed in. I never did get the hang of them, but just pushed and pulled at random while pedalling away for dear life. O death! Where is thy sting?

Long before my time worshippers in Scottish kirks considered the kist o' whustles a noisy wheezy instrument which shattered their Sunday peace. They were accustomed to a precentor who pinged his tuning fork to find the right note and sang over the first verse by himself. At least, I didn't have to do *that*.

In those bygone days it was thought sacrilege for choirs to rehearse the psalms in their Biblical words. So at choir practices they were given substitute verses, or just made them up as they went along. I thought some of the Biblical words were silly enough.

> Like as the hart for water-brooks
> In thirst doth pant and bray;
> So pants my longing soul, O God,
> That come to Thee I may.

I thought the secular version was far jollier.

> I gaed an' keekit up the lum
> The skies for to behold;
> A daud o' soot fell in ma e'e,
> Which did me quite blindfold.

Though I was no volunteer organist I had to play a solemn piece called a voluntary at the beginning of the service. This was supposed to set the mood while the congregation settled down and Leckie, the beadle, carried the big Bible up the pulpit stairs before leading in the minister. It was not easy to time, for I had to play on till His Reverence sat down and said his own private prayer before I could bring my piece to a suitable conclusion that sounded like an amen.

Even worse was the piece I had to play in the middle while the collection was being taken and folk were fumbling in their pooches for their offerings. I had to keep an eye in the back of my head to see when the elders came marching forward, carrying the offerings on brass plates to set before the minister, after solemnly bowing to him.

Often I was left high and dry in the middle of nowhere and had to improvise a hasty ending. Then there was the final piece when the kirk was scaling, which had to have a more joyful sound like a hallelujah, thank goodness it's over.

Finding suitable pieces for these performances brought many a furrow to my brow. Sometimes I just made them up as I went along. *Thumb*-one-two-three! But I had to be careful not to stray into 'Caller Herrin'' or the 'Laird o' Cockpen' by mistake. It was now that Handel and his mournful Largo came into his own. I even culled *Hemy's*

Tutor to see if 'Le Carnavel de Venise', played extra slow, would pass muster.

'Was that not "Come into the Garden, Maud" you were playing?' the minister once accused me in the vestry after a service.

'It could have been. I wasn't listening.'

Some of the congregation had music in their hymn books and kept looking at it knowingly to let everyone see they could read the doh-ray-me's. I had my favourite hates among the hymns. 'O love that wilt not let me go-oh!' went rambling on for ever. Sometimes I slipped in a few twiddly-bits to relieve the monotony. And I always wanted to shout 'Yes!' when the minister announced that we would sing: 'Art thou weary, art thou languid?'

It was difficult to keep a straight face when Mrs Stout stood up in the choir, bursting out of her costume, and announced to the congregation that she was a little pilgrim. It made a change from 'Hail Caledonia', and one blessing was there were no encores.

All the same, I had good reason to be grateful to Mrs Stout and her girth.

It happened on my first Sunday as reluctant organist. They were all bad, but that was the worst day of all. I still have the shudders when I think of it.

Out of mistaken kindness and in honour of the occasion Mrs Leckie, the beadle's wife, had polished the waxcloth underneath the organ stool with some new and extra-slippery polish. I got through the first paraphrase somehow, but when I began to play 'By cool Siloam's shady rill' I suddenly realized I was on the move. Backwards.

I was so horror-stricken I bit my lip till it bled, but that did not help my predicament. Nothing I could do would prevent the stool from slipping and sliding farther away from the organ. I had to keep on bicycling though I could scarcely stretch out my feet to reach the pedals. Nor my hands to reach the keyboard. If I kept going backwards I would be left in midair miming the music. Siloam's rills may have been shady, but the perspiration was trickling down my backbone.

It was the little pilgrim who came to my rescue. Mrs Stout saw my plight, and when she rose to sing the first verse stationed herself immediately behind me and dunted me back towards the organ. I kept coming and going but never, thank goodness, got past the Rock of Gibraltar.

Sometimes she dunted me too far and too fast, so that I was rushed towards the kist o' whustles, almost winding myself when I got banged in the stomach. Mrs Stout, poor soul, got hit, too, on her hindquarters when I went scooshing back; but what did a few bruises matter compared with saving the situation? There were six verses in cool Siloam (none omitted) but they seemed millions to me. By the time I played amen I felt as if I had been hung, drawn and quartered; and I noticed that Mrs Stout sat down very gingerly in her chair.

The rest of the choir, consisting mainly of Bob Somebody who sang high, Jim Somebody who sang low, and a big man who was neither one thing nor the other, got the message and stretched out their feet to act as brakes when I had to play while the offerings were being collected. And during the rest of the service they stood in strategic positions, taking some of the strain off Mrs Stout who had shot her bolt.

I thanked her profusely afterwards and would have invested her there and then with the VC. I also thanked Mrs Leckie for polishing the linoleum but begged her NEVER to do it again. I had enough worries without that.

There were occasions while I was playing that I noticed the minister flinching, but he wasn't perfect either. Once he led the whole congregation through 'The Lord's My Shepherd' instead of Our Father, and forever after kept The Lord's Prayer written out in large letters to keep him on the straight and narrow.

He was above me, in more ways than one, half hidden by a vase of flowers. One Sunday in a fit of exuberance he flailed out his arms while winding up his discourse and knocked the whole jingbang down on top of me. To do me credit, I never turned a hair though I was sopping wet and strewn with wilting gladioli. I did hope the Lord was looking so that He could put a good mark against my name in His golden jotter.

I could sometimes twist H.J.'s arm when I couldn't play a certain hymn or paraphrase. 'Could we not just have "Gentle Jesus?" ' I would plead with him in the vestry before the service. It was a different matter if a visiting minister came with a list of hymns I had never heard of, which suited the theme of his sermon, and which he insisted on my playing.

I am unlikely to forget the day when H.J. had to exchange pulpits with a preacher from Duns, a severe gentleman who never smiled on the Sabbath day. Or any other day, I suspected. I was more worried about what to give him for lunch till he handed me the praise list in the vestry. Not one of them had I seen before.

'Oh, I don't think . . .' I began. Then, after one look at his face, I knew that even if I went down on my bended knees before him, he would not change it. We were all at sixes and sevens, but fortunately he liked the sound of his own loud voice, and led the praise himself in true precentor style. His last amen must certainly have been heard in heaven.

'I thought the singing was excellent,' he said afterwards in the Manse, as he was passing in his plate for a second helping of steak pie. Meaning: 'Wasn't *I* excellent?'

'Yes!' I said, dumping a spoonful of turnips on his plate and restraining myself from throwing it at him. At least, thank goodness, he drowned out the organ.

When Miss Steele came back with a brand-new inside – O happy day! – the kirk session wanted to make me a presentation for my pains. Pains was the right word; but I said No! I had everything I wanted. And so I had. The best present of all: freedom to leave the kist o' whustles and return to the sanctuary of my box-pew.

9. The Brethren

But many of these episodes were still to come . . .

Before all that happened, when the sleeping beauty awoke she turned out to be more like an ugly sister. The Manse garden had sour soil.

'Soor!' said Leckie, the Tattie-Bogle, shaking a spadeful of compost on a flowerbed as if sprinkling sugar over a pudding.

But the weeds flourished. In odd moments I did my share of howking them out; and found it fascinating to see what would blossom next, in spite of the poor soil. After the snowdrops came the daffodils and primroses, followed in due course by a variety of spring flowers. The Major's wife could have named them all specifically. There were some nice bushes of rhododendrons which Leckie called 'Roddydandrums', and a fine display of dandelions and thistles.

The auld meenister had not been much of a gardener. Neither was the new meenister, though he sometimes laid down his fiddle and came out to pick up a hoe. But soon he laid that down, too, and began practising the long jump on the lawn, watched admiringly by Wee Wullie and disapprovingly by old Miss Calder keeking over the hedge.

The hens had begun to lay, there was a tang of spring in the air, and who could blame H.J. for feeling frisky. When I went out to collect the eggs I wanted to kick up my heels and turn somersaults, as I would have done if I had been in the meadow at home. 'Watch it! Put on the brakes!' I had to warn myself. So it was Wee Wullie who turned the somersaults instead. In between helping God to hoe the garden.

'Would you not like to go and play?' I asked him one day, seeing a laddie hanging about at the gate waiting for him.

'No' wi' *him*!' scoffed Wee Wullie.

'Why not?'

'He's too young.'

'Oh! How much younger than you?'

'A day,' said Wee Wullie.

It made all the difference.

I felt quite young myself in the spring air when I could escape from the rigours of running the Manse. Sometimes a great longing came over me for the carefree freedom of life on the farm. The only remedy was to work it off in the kitchen, or walk it off with my collecting book. Sometimes I took the puppy with me on a lead and wandered cross-country to visit one of the remote cottages, combining duty with pleasure.

The countryside was flatter than my own Borderland, with undulations rather than hills, yet there were familiar sights to see. Drystane dykes, which I climbed rather than search for a gate, a discarded bath lying in a field, a lamb 'taigled' in a briar. I knew how to disentangle it, and how to set a whummled sheep right way up when I came across one lying helpless on its back with feet in the air.

But there were unfamiliar notices to be seen. 'No Road This Way' and 'Trespassers will be Prosecuted'. I kept Bush at my heels and was careful not to step out of line.

One day I saw a shepherd and his dog advancing towards me. For a moment I thought it was Jock-the-herd and my heart gave a leap till he shouted at me. 'D'ye no' ken ye're trespassin'?' Then, recognizing me, he touched his cap and stopped for a 'speak'.

As he leant on his crook we discussed yowes and gimmers and tups and braxie and loupin'-ill. All the things I was familiar with through Jock-the-herd. It was the first sensible conversation I had had for ages.

Then one day I saw a familiar figure shambling across a field, swiping at thistles with his stick and roaring threats to the sky. Yorkie, the tramp, who was a frequent caller at our farmhouse.

Though I was always half frightened of Yorkie, he was a link with home and I rushed forward to greet him, but he just gave me a wild gaze, mumbled something and pushed past. Had he recognized me, I wondered? No use asking *him* anything. 'Have you been to Overton Bush lately? Did you sleep in the byre or the barn? What did you get to eat?' He was well on his way, fending off imaginary assailants with his stick.

The vagrants who roamed the countryside with no fixed abode were constant callers at the Manse, as they had been at the farmhouse. I never turned any away and gave them what I could to eat, but I missed the garret at home where I could nip up and find an old jacket or a pair of cast-off trousers. The minister and I needed every

garment we possesed, though sometimes I was tempted
to give away his carpet slippers or my own shoes to an
old crone who said, 'See! I'm walkin' on ma uppers.'

I boiled an egg for her tea to make up for it, but she
couldn't walk on *that*.

All the same, was I growing harder?

It was the scroungers I disliked with their glib hard-up
stories, who would not be fobbed off with me but
demanded to see His Reverence. 'God bless Your
Holiness. May he have mercy on your soul, and can you
spare a shilling for a poor old sinner?'

Sometimes it was a poor young sinner who insinuated
his way into the study and held His Holiness at bay with
some cock-and-bull story. H.J. was a soft touch and
always fell for it.

'Give him the benefit of the doubt,' he would say.

Well, yes! We were supposed to show a Christian
example in the Manse, but I hated being taken in and was
sure I could spot the wrong ones. Sometimes I went
barging into the study on some pretext and gave H.J. a
warning look, to interrupt one of these encounters just as
the minister, looking shamefaced, was putting his hand
in his pocket.

To his credit he never complained when the inevitable
happened and he found he had been fooled. And to my
credit I never humiliated him by saying, 'I told you so!'

It was his kingdom, not mine. I was only an appen-
dage, but it was at such times I felt older and wiser than
my brother. The truth was, though *he* had been out in the
world, we were both raw. But if H.J. made one mistake,
I made hundreds. Yet, I tried to back him up in all he was
doing, even if it was only to say 'Uh-huh!' when he came
in complaining of how busy he was.

He never poured out his heart to me, but he wrote
regularly to Mother telling of his progress, and she sent

back long fond letters to Sonny. Occasionally I enclosed a scrawl inside one of his, just a plain statement of what I had been doing that week. I came across one recently. It read like an assault course. Just re-reading it exhausted me. The ending was always the same. 'Love to Jessie and Jock-the-herd.' When I thought of home, it was of them.

Feeling instinctively that he needed reassurance, I tried to say something encouraging to H.J. now and then. 'That was a good sermon.' Or: 'Well done!' But we were not good at praising each other . I would have fallen down in a dead faint if *he* had said, 'That wasn't a bad scone,' or, 'The soup's quite good.' If he passed his plate for more, I took that as a compliment.

There was little doubt he had conquered the hearts of his parishioners both in and out of the pulpit. But there was another august body he wanted to impress. The brethren. Older and wiser ministers from neighbouring parishes who congregated now and again, like hoodie crows, to discuss – what? The Schemes of the Church?

H.J. was always on tenterhooks when he set out to attend one of their meetings. I could tell when he came back and picked up his fiddle how the deliberations had gone. If he played a rousing Scots reel, all was well, but if it sounded like the 'Dead March in Saul' I gave him an extra sausage for his supper.

Once in a while the brethren held unofficial gatherings in each others' Manses, and, after discussing the affairs of the kirk, they partook of a high tea provided by their hostess; the higher the better, for they did not live by bread alone. They liked fancy cakes as well. All the reverends had hearty appetites and looked forward to a good spread following their deliberations.

The Lady of the Manse, of course, was not permitted to join their meeting. Her place was in the kitchen preparing the feast, but she was graciously permitted to

preside at the tea pouring in the dining room afterwards.
It was a great honour for her to be feeding so many godly
men.

The Manse ladies vied with each other to provide a
groaning board. It was my turn to groan when the lot fell
on Jonah. If ever I wanted to run away, it was on that day
when the hoodie crows, some seventeen of them,
descended on the doorstep.

H.J. was like 'a hen on a het girdle', as Jessie would
have said, not settling to anything but being a perfect
nuisance to me and Oor Net who were stretched to our
limits, like frayed elastic. He was in and out of the kitchen
a dozen times, not doing anything but asking anxiously,
'Are you sure you've thought of everything?'

'Yes, I'm sure!' I said, wishing he had taken up any
other 'trade' than the ministry, even burglary. 'We're
getting on fine.'

(Not true; but I had enough on my plate without
coping with his nerves as well.)

'Away and play the fiddle,' I suggested.

No, he couldn't do that. He would just run up to the
drawing room to see if the fire was burning. I had just run
up myself and slid back down the bannisters; but I let him
go to keep him occupied while Nettie and I set the
dining-room table and counted the chairs.

I had been at it for days. Years, it seemed. Cleaning,
polishing, dusting and baking everything I could think
of. My first batch of rock cakes lived up to their names,
but I baked a new lot and the back door tramps ate the
others. I made sausage rolls, dropscones, plain scones,
currant scones, shortbread, tarts, little buns which I iced,
a big cut-and-come again cake and Jessie's gingerbread
which had no recipe.

I had to ring up the farmhouse to find out.

'Can I speak to Jessie, please?' I asked urgently.

'What is't?' she said sharply.

'Jessie! Tell me what you put into your gingerbread.'

'Intil't? Toots!' said Jessie, flummoxed.

She never weighed anything out. ('A wee tait o' this, an' a wee tait o' that.') But at least she told me the ingredients and I had a shot at it. It was not too bad, but not a patch on Jessie's. I even bought chocolate biscuits from the housekeeping money which was at its usual low ebb, and made meringues which tasted all right, though they looked a bit lopsided. I hoped there would be something left over, else we would starve for the rest of the week.

Long before we were ready the doorbell rang.

'Michty God!' exclaimed Oor Net, getting it out of her system before the reverends came in. She was engaged in a tricky operation, trying to make butterballs. She had to dip the butterbats into a jug of boiling water, then roll the butter round and round till it made a perfect circle, but as usual she was getting both herself and the butter in a fankle. 'Damnation! I'm no' dressed. I haveny got on ma clean pinny.'

'I'll go,' I said, abandoning the cream I was whipping for the meringues and wiping some of it off my nose. 'It might not be them.'

It wasn't. It was Aileen on the doorstep with her dog, Jasper. 'I was wondering,' she said gently, 'if you'd like to come for a walk, if you're not doing anything.' Then, seeing my flushed face: 'Oh! Are you busy?'

'Well, sort of! Another day.'

'Yes,' she said, understanding, and turned away. Oh jings! Wouldn't it have been bliss to have gone with her?

We were ready for the brethren when they arrived. The Manse had never looked so spick and span. I had even tidied my bedroom, though, goodness knows! I didn't expect any of the hoodie crows in there. The study was unrecognizable. Not a golf ball or a crumpled *Sporting Times* in sight. And the drawing room where the crows were to congregate looked welcoming, with the fire burning brightly, and a vase of flowers on the piano. But the dining room when the table was spread was the *pièce de résistance*.

'Holy Moses! Will they they eat all *that*?' gasped Oor Net when she saw the spread assembled on the table.

Even H.J. admitted it was not bad.

He stationed himself at the door, with Nettie, in clean pinny, hovering in the background. I stayed out of sight and kept the kettles boiling. Wee Wullie, looking scared to death, was at the back door. One God he could cope with – but seventeen! I sent him off with Bush for a walk and gave him a squashy meringue to eat on the way.

Nettie and I took turns to creep halfway up the stairs and listen like conspirators to find out when the meeting was drawing to a close, and we would have to mask the tea.

'That's them feenished!' said Oor Net, scurrying into the kitchen. 'Some o' them's went to the bathroom.'

I was waiting for them in the dining room when they came down, rubbing their newly washed hands and looking hungrily at the spread on the table. I had had to borrow cups from Mrs Sturrock and a teapot from Miss Calder in the Loaning. 'You'll take good care of it. It's Georgian,' she warned me. Then inquisitively: 'You wouldn't like me to come and pour out?'

'No, I wouldn't,' I said firmly. I would reward her with some rock cakes, if there were any left.

So I did the pouring out myself, after greeting the brethren, some of whom I knew already, and getting them seated at the table. I had the Georgian teapot poised when the most venerable of the crows launched into a long grace. Oor Net, standing behind me with the hot-water jug, closed her eyes reverently. I hoped she would not deluge me with boiling water while he prayed not only for me, but for her. 'Our handmaiden.'

Luckily, she said 'Amen' at the end, not 'Holy Moses!', and we were off.

The brethrens' hands met in midstream as they stretched out to help themselves, and I was kept fully occupied filling and refilling their cups with occasional rushes to the kitchen.

'More scones, please, Nettie.'

'Michty God!'

It was as well she was out of earshot.

They came in all shapes and sizes. The brethren, as well as the scones. With the inevitable joker who fancied himself as a comic. 'Do not be so disconsolate at having to take a soda scone so late,' said he, passing a plate to his neighbour. (I had heard that one a thousand times!) And the complimentary ones, passing comments after each bite. 'Delicious cake, this!' (You should have seen it before I scraped its burnt bottom!)

They talked between mouthfuls, not of holy matters, but of the food. 'Try another meringue. They melt in the mouth.'

The brethren never addressed me as a grown-up person. (Of course, I wasn't.) The jokey one focused his wit in my direction. It would not have surprised me if he had done tricks. Made his handkie vanish up his sleeve, as Father used to do to amuse me. 'Shut up! You old bore!'

Yet, they were all good men and true, all doing noble work in their parishes, struggling – as we were – to make ends meet. All with families to rear and their own problems to solve, as well as their parishioners'. Why should they not loosen their waistcoats once in a while and enjoy a good tuck-in?

You, you and you! I thought, looking round the table when I had a breather. You must each have a secret life of your own. How did you hear the call, and was it the right sound? And do you truly believe everything the Bible says? The comic, sharing the last meringue with his neighbour – is your dearest wish to play the harp in heaven?

I could see by the expression on H.J.'s face that things were going well, though he had not enough gumption to ignore the empty platters and asked, 'Are there any more meringues?'

'I'll see,' I said, giving him a withering look, and knowing full well there were none.

I hurried to the kitchen and filled the plate with odds and ends of shortbread and cast-off rock cakes.

At long last everyone had had their fill. Some of the brethren sat back and filled their pipes, and the jokey one declared he was fit to burst. I could have dived below the table when a little fat one got up to make a speech aimed at our charming young hostess. Me! ('Shut up! Shut up!') But he patted his well-filled kite and went on extolling my virtues. A lot of nonsense.

I hated the speech but I liked the box of chocolates he suddenly produced from under his jacket. Nettie and I devoured them while washing the dishes. They helped to take away the taste of that awful afternoon, but it was a high price to pay.

H.J. went and played some jigs on the fiddle. He'd had a hard enough day without helping with the dishes!

'Michty God!' said Oor Net, popping a chocolate cream into her mouth with a soapy hand before washing yet another empty plate. 'They fairly went their dingers, thon meenisters. It's a blessin' there's some plain breid left.'

She had gone home and I was polishing Miss Calder's Georgian teapot when H.J. popped his head round the kitchen door.

'What's for supper?' he asked hungrily.

Holy Moses! I thought. It'll have to be scrambled eggs on toast.

Eventually I got my walk with Aileen.

'How do you cope?' she asked sympathetically.

'Not very well. Don't let's talk about it.'

We talked instead about writing, and she became almost animated as we discussed the ups and downs of our literary careers. Well, hardly careers! My writing was done in stolen moments, mostly late at night, and was more down to earth, more slapdash than Aileen's.

She would spend hours polishing one sentence till she rubbed all the sparkle out of it, and out of herself. Then she had to lie down, exhausted, on the chaise longue in her writing room.

I tried to pep her up, acting like cod-liver oil, and was pleased to see some colour in her cheeks and more spring to her step.

How often we wandered the back lanes talking about acceptances and rejections, and how often I had to turn on my heel and say, 'Help! I must run!'

Sir Joseph and Lady Victoria, seeking to encourage this strange friendship, invited me to 'drop in for midmorning sherry'. I had more mundane things to do midmorning, but I went once when H.J. had gone to join the brethren at a presbytery meeting.

The Lady was wearing a flowerpot hat and Sir Joseph dispensed sherry as if serving royalty. I was unaccustomed to any drink stronger than communion wine, but I sipped away and tried not to be too tongue-tied.

Didn't I think Darling was looking better? 'Oh yes, much!' But she mustn't overstrain herself working too hard at her writing. 'No, no; she mustn't!' As for myself, was I taking care of my own health? 'Oh yes, great care!'

It was better when Aileen took me upstairs to see her writing room. It was then that I saw the maid dusting the pens and pencils on her desk. She bobbed a curtsey and withdrew when we came in. I wondered if I could get Oor Net to treat me with such deference. Aileen showed me her treasures, the piece that had been printed in *Punch*, the notes she was trying to compile for her book on Nell Gwyn, her reference books, and a poem she had begun but never ended.

'I'm waiting for inspiration,' she said, sinking down on the chaise longue.

'Och! you might wait for ever,' I said briskly. 'Why not have a shot at something else meantime?'

'What?' she asked vaguely.

'Well, why not an article on walking the dog? Think of all the things you see in the lanes, and the capers Jasper gets up to . . .' I had it all mapped out for her by the time I left. And as she walked me to the gate, she said, 'Oh yes! I'll try it. I'll start this afternoon. After I've had my rest.'

As I hurried back to the Manse I thought ahead to my own afternoon. Visit Mrs Somebody and her bad leg. Guild meeting. Back to the Manse to do the ironing and prepare the minister's supper. Pump up that infernal machine for hot water. Do the darning. Help! Was this rehearsal night for a forthcoming concert?

In spite of it all, I did not envy Aileen. Not really! I would have hated spending half my life lying on a sofa. But it was nice knowing her, nice that we had so much in common, and that there was *someone* I could tell when *Life and Work* accepted an article on the life and work of a Manse lady.

Wee Wullie was whistling at the back door. One of the minister's tunes. I stopped to listen. There was no doubt the laddie had an ear for music. Perfect pitch. I knew what *his* dearest wish was, and remembered there was an old fiddle in the garret at home.

Wait, Wullie, wait! Maybe your dream will come true.

10. Berwick Cockles

Sarah Googly said to me, 'I've never had a nicer present in a' ma born days. Losh! Lassie, ye're a bobbydazzler!'

To be a bobbydazzler was high praise. It brought a flush to my cheeks, and I wondered why we Borderers didn't pay compliments more often. Of course, I spoiled it by saying, 'Oh, it's nothing!' (Another of our weaknesses. Why couldn't we accept a compliment gracefully?) 'I just made it out of odds and ends.'

True; but the shawl I had knitted for old Sarah out of odds and ends of wool and in all the colours of the rainbow did look nice when she put it round her shoulders. Like Jacob's coat of many colours. I had sat up in bed the night before to finish it in time, ganting between the rows. Ganting? Jessie's word for yawning.

It was Sarah Googly's eighty-eighth birthday, or it could have been her ninetieth. She was not sure, but her

114

daughter Kate – Mistress Niven – knew the date, if not the year, and had laid on a little teaparty to mark the occasion, held ben the hoose in the best room, complete with silver sugar tongs, lace doyleys on the plates, and a birthday cake with one candle in the middle.

I would sooner have been in the sweetie shop leaning on the counter and chatting to old Sarah on my own, but this was an occasion. It would have crowned the occasion if the minister had been able to come, but he was away at one of his meetings, so Mistress Niven had to put up with me. She held her pinky high while sipping her tea, the picture of gentility, and engaged me in meaningless small talk till old Sarah broke in.

'I wanted to ask the meenister a question. What'll happen to me when I'm deid? Will I gang straight up or straight doon? Or will I hover for a wee while till the Lord makes up His mind? Eh whowh!'

I had often pondered the problem myself, but I answered light-heartedly, breaking into braid Scots. 'Hoots! We'll a' be deid lang afore you, Sarah!' Then, more seriously: 'I tell you what, I'll ask the minister to drop in and you can talk about it together.'

'Ay, you do that, lassie.'

On my way back to the Manse I wished I could eavesdrop on their conversation, and wondered why *I* could never talk to the minister about such fundamental matters. He would have been very embarrassed, I felt sure, and so would I. I could say to him, 'Please pass the marmalade,' but if I said, 'Please tell me what heaven's like,' he would have taken a turn.

I knew what he had taken right now! The one and only Manse key after locking the door behind him. It happened quite often, so I was not unduly disturbed. I could easily do my cat burglar act, hoisting myself on to the study window ledge, pushing up the window and diving headfirst into the room.

Undetected, I hoped. But not today.

'Can I be of any assistance?'

I knew that quiet voice. It belonged to the Pisky Parson, Mr Montrose, from the Episcopalian church up the road.

> Pisky! pisky, A-men!
> Doon on your knees an' up again!

A heathen church according to many of the Presbyterian diehards.

The brethren had little time for the Pisky Parson though he was preaching the same gospel, only in a different way. And surely the Lord did not favour the Scots kirk more than the English church; or, for that matter, the Hottentots. Though I remember old Mrs Eliot from the village at home declaring she was sure Jesus was a Borderer. Hawick, she favoured as His habitation on earth.

I was sorry for the Pisky Parson because he had a club foot and found it difficult to hirple about without the aid of a stick. How did he manage to get up and down on his knees, I wondered?

Some of the gentry went to his church for early morning services called matins, and evensong at night. It all sounded strange and romantic to me, though the Pisky Parson himself was no heartthrob. He had an unkempt air about him, like a shaggy dog who needed a good brush-up. He was a scholar, it was said, so maybe he had a mind above brushes and combs.

Any time we met on the road he stopped to rest his foot and have a word with me. Not about scholarly things, just the weather. Now here he was getting a less dignified view of me.

'Can't I give you a hand?'

'No, no, Mr Montrose. It's all right. The minister's gone off with the doorkey, but I can manage fine, thank you. I'm used to it. Goodnight!'

And with that I dived in through the window.

Bush was barking with boredom and the telephone ringing.

'Shut up!' I said to the puppy and 'Hullo!' to the telephone.

It was Mrs Sturrock asking if I would take part in the Dramatics.

'What's that?'

'Plays.'

'Oh! But I can't act for toffee.'

'Never mind. You'll do fine. I'll put your name down,' said Mrs Sturrock and rang off.

She didn't add, 'It'll give you something to do,' but that's what she meant.

But before that I was to see some real acting.

Next day H.J. and I were playing hooky, driving to Berwick, and going to the talking pictures. I had seen the silent pictures in Jedburgh. Even they were a treat to me, but the talkies! What would it be like to hear someone speak on the screen? There was also going to be some singing and dancing. All talking, all singing, all dancing! Something to do with Broadway. And in a picture house as grand as a palace, with a wurlitzer, even finer than the Major's pianola, and cushioned seats to sit on.

Very different from the hard benches in the Jedburgh town hall, where a flickering screen was erected once in a while for the silent pictures. Not so silent! There was a constant hubbub of sound. Handclapping, jeering when the film broke down, exclamations of delight or horror as we followed the fate of the film stars to the accompaniment of little Miss Somebody playing soulful or hurry-up music on a tinkling piano. But it was magical, for all that. I remember walking eight miles from the farm to see Pola Negri, and eight miles back, never noticing that my legs ached.

Now I was going to the talkies in style, driving in the Baby Austin across the frontier into England.

I felt a little guilty at leaving Oor Net to hold the fort.

'Don't work too hard,' I admonished her.

'No, I'll not,' she promised. I was sure she would keep her word.

The Pisky Parson waved to me as we passed him in the Village street. 'Him!' said H.J., changing gear. What was wrong with the poor man? Surely he was as good as any of the brethren. I waved to Aileen coming out of the post office with Jasper at her heels. I hoped she had finished her article and was posting it off to a newspaper. And that it wouldn't come back!

Mr Sturrock, the lugubrious elder, looked even more long-faced when he saw the minister driving past in soft collar and cloth cap. A turn of the corner and we were on the Great North Road, shaking off the shackles and following the fascinating coastline that led to Berwick-upon-Tweed.

It was a great build-up to the treat that lay ahead. I liked to sit silent and not have things pointed out to me, so I was content enough to see what I could with my own eyes. And when we reached Berwick itself, with its bridges and gates, its huddled red roofs, its walls and ramparts, its crowded streets and wynds, I felt as if I was stepping through history.

H.J. went off to purchase some sermon paper, and I stood like a stookie outside the picture house gaping at everything.

The street market was on, and they were selling everything from a needle to an anchor; though, truthfully I saw neither. But there were jugs, mugs, pillowcases, sheets, curtains, cheap jewellery, clogs, carpet slippers, bootlaces and kettles. There was some material that I might have made into a frock, but I had no money to spare. So I listened instead to a man shouting his wares and making comical quips in a Geordie accent. He was giving away great bargains, so he said; cases of knives and forks, with an alarum clock thrown in, to the lucky hinnies who put up their hands.

I kept mine firmly clenched, sensing he was a phoney like some of the chancers who called at the Manse to touch His Holiness for money. Yet he was amusing, and it was great to stand there untrammelled, taking in all the sights and sounds. Maybe I could put my impressions down on paper some day.

'Come on! It's time we went in.'

H.J. loomed up beside me, clutching his sermon paper and a small poke of Berwick cockles which he had thoughtfully provided; and soon I was transported from one fascinating scene to another.

The minister ate all the cockles himself. I was far too engrossed and would not have noticed if I was dying of starvation. I was away in Hollywood with the beautiful people. They never felt cold or hungry, never had blemishes on their faces, bunions on their feet, or colds in their heads. They were perpetually smiling, showing their perfect teeth. I smiled with them, pleased to see them all so happy. Who wanted reality?

It was great to see such perfection. Not a hair out of place, not a fingernail unmanicured, not a wrinkle in their stockings or on their brows. Their frilly petticoats were snow-white when they twirled in the dance. Never, never did they soil their hands at the kitchen sink. They were too busy singing, dancing, and making love.

The man at the mighty organ came up from nowhere

and played stirring music interspersed with haunting melodies that still kept me floating on a high level.

At the end – a happy ending, thank goodness! – I breathed a sigh of satisfaction. And exhaustion. I had been through so many emotions. I could have sat on for ever, but H.J. was on his feet so I followed him out, blinking in the daylight.

The market folk were folding up their wares, the funny man clinking his coins as he counted them. We went to the Green Café for tea and buns and gradually came down from the heights.

H.J. reverted to 'the minister' and began looking at the scribbles in his diary, fussing about all he had to do in the next few weeks.

'Wait!' I pleaded inwardly. 'Let me stay up here a while longer.'

But he was mumbling into his coffee bun. 'Bazaar! They thought about getting you to open it, but decided to have somebody more important.' (Bless them!) 'Annie S. Swan.'

'Oh, good!'

She was a writer, the most popular authoress in Scotland. Her stories were read in every cot and castle in the land. It would be interesting meeting her.

On the way home the Baby broke down but I didn't mind a bit. When the engine started to hiccup I got out automatically and started to shove. I wondered if the Broadway beauties had ever heaved a car out of a ditch. Perhaps they were only human, like me, but I doubted it. I preferred to think of them twirling on their toes without a care in the world. We all needed glamour in our lives, even if it was someone else's.

Oor Net had left a note on the kitchen table, written on brown paper with a stub of pencil.

'The soap's done. Miss Calder has came and went. A

man called about selling something. He's coming back tomorra. Sorry I've broke the blue bowel.'

Back to normal.

Next day there was to be a wedding in the Manse.

I was to become accustomed to these occasions when an uneasy-looking foursome would arrive at the front door: the bride and groom with their best maid and best man, looking as if they were going to their execution.

Usually they were whispering nervously to each other, the men fingering their collars, the women easing their feet in their split-new shoes. The men wore navy-blue suits and the women their good costumes, with hats stuck at the back of their heads and a wee veil fluttering over their eyes. It was difficult to tell which was the happy couple. They all wore flowers in their lapels. Carnations were the favourites with a frond of gypsophila to set them off, though sometimes it was artificial roses or even sprigs of holly, depending on the season of the year.

The engaged pair had paid preliminary visits to the minister and he had talked to them solemnly in the study. Then their banns had been called in church.

'There is a purpose of marriage between Jean Riddell, spinster of this parish, and John Pringle, bachelor . . .'

So everyone knew their intentions in advance. And those who did not want to face up to a church wedding came to the Manse to finalize their vows in the drawing room.

On that first occasion Oor Net and I went to great lengths to make the room look festive. I gathered as many flowers and as much greenery as I could find, and tried to make a garland to place on top of the piano, but it kept tumbling down. However, though it looked a bit of a mess, it took the bareness away.

'Have we no' got naethin' to chuck at them?' asked Nettie.

'Like what?'

'Confetti.'

No! I did not keep confetti in the cupboard along with such necessities as treacle and bathbrick.

'It'll have to be rice, if anything,' I told her. But we had run out of rice so we had to settle for lentils. Oor Net had a fistful ready long before the deed was done.

The minister put on his good blacks and his dog collar to do the deed properly. I hoped he didn't expect me to play 'Here Comes the Bride' and he didn't.

'Just take them up to the drawing room and keep out of the way,' he told me.

But Oor Net and I wanted to be in at the kill. She knew Jean Riddell (soon to be Mrs John Pringle) and was almost as excited as the bride herself. 'She was in the top class at school when I was in the Infants. Fancy!'

I tried to be bright about it when I greeted the foursome on the doorstep.

'This is a very happy day,' said I, welcoming them in.

'I doot it'll turn to rain,' said the bridegroom dolefully, or it could have been the best man.

The bride and her maid were still whispering to each other as we ascended the stairs. About their sore feet? I left them standing in a huddle on the hearthrug, and slid down the bannisters.

'All set!' I told the minister, and he mounted the stairs, bible in hand.

Nettie and I, cocking our lugs, could hear various rumblings from above, then suddenly the drawing room door opened and it was all over. The minister led the way downstairs, smiling. The foursome followed, looking as relieved as if they had come out of the dentist's. We all shook hands with them and wished them luck. Oor Net let fly with her handful of lentils and scored a direct hit on the minister. Then away they went, linking arms, to have a 'wee celebration'.

I hoped the minister had married the right couple.

(It was strange in after-years to be stopped by mature women who said, 'Oh, hullo! Did you know your brother married me?' As if I had hundreds of sisters-in-law!

I soon grew accustomed to such intrusions into the Manse privacy. (What privacy?) I learned to take them for granted, carrying on with my usual chores but keeping a stock of rice handy in the cupboard. Now and again there was a deviation from the set pattern.

One day when I was chopping onions for the stew and a foursome were up in the drawing room being 'done', I was aware of a strange sound outside the kitchen door.

'Psssst!'

It was the minister trying to attract my attention.

'What is't?' I asked, wiping away my oniony tears.

'Have you got a ring?' he asked urgently.

'What kind of ring?'

'A wedding ring,' he said impatiently.

'I'm not married . . .'

'Don't be so daft! Any kind of ring'll do. The best man's forgotten it. Silly sumph!'

After a great deal of hunting in the kitchen drawers I came across a curtain ring.

'That'll do,' said H.J., and promptly dropped it on the floor.

'Silly sumph!' I said under my breath, and picked it up for him.

After that I kept a cheap ring, bought at a jumble sale, in a handy place for emergencies. As well as a glass of water and a bottle of smelling salts on the piano after a bridegroom had come over queer and collapsed at his bride's feet.

It was the men, I found, who took turns and the women who propped them up. They had had a hard enough job getting their swains as far as the Manse and were not going to let them off the hook now. 'Stand up, Tam! Ye've got to gang through wi't.' There was no escape.

One time I had to stand in as best maid and we got the postie who was passing to act as best man.

'I could pit on a moustache, if ye're stuck,' Oor Net had volunteered, but she had to stick to her humbler task of rice thrower.

She was thrilled, though, about Annie S. Swan coming to open the Bazaar.

'Holy Moses! Ma mother'll be aff her heid. She's read the *Friend* since she was a lassie. Me, tae! Jings Geordie! Fancy meetin' her! Ye should read some o' her stories. They're tremenjus. Awful like the thing. Whiles they're a bit sad, but ma mother likes a wee greet. It cheers her up.'

To cheer me up Nettie brought me a copy of the *People's Friend* and that night, after she had gone home, I leant my elbows on the kitchen table to have a wee read, if not a wee greet.

It was good wholesome stuff and I could see the pull it had in so many country households. Indeed, I became so absorbed that I drew in a chair and sat down to it.

It was some time before I became aware of a tap-tapping at the back door.

'Come in,' I called, thinking it was Wee Wullie; but when I heard a pug yapping I knew it was Miss Calder from the Loaning.

She looked at me disapprovingly.

'Have you nothing better to do than sit and read all day?'

'No, nothing,' said I, looking up at her in a daze. I was still away with Annie S. Swan. Would Alison Lowrie marry that nice doctor?

'What are you reading?' Miss Calder asked inquisitively. I tried to conceal the paper with my elbow, but she saw it. 'That rubbish!'

'It's not rubbish!' I said, hotly defending Annie S. Swan. But she was no longer listening.

'I see the minister's car's not in the garage, so you'll have to come and sort the bedroom window. It's got stuck.'

It was a royal command, so I had to abandon Alison Lowrie and trail away after her.

Never mind! The story, when I did manage to finish it, had a happy ending. Alison did marry the nice doctor. I liked happy endings, even if they were not in real life.

11. The Bazaar

I was drinking a glass of my favourite beverage, soor dook, in the farmhouse kitchen at home, sitting on the table dangling my legs. As usual I had helped Jessie with the kirning, now I was reaping my reward.

'Nae mair, lassie, or ye'll droon,' she warned me.

'Oh! It's so good,' I said, licking my lips. Better than Sir Joseph's sherry.

But everything tasted better here. I sniffed the appetizing smells coming from the pots on the fire. When I cooked the same stews and stovies at the Manse they never gave out such mouthwatering aromas. There was an apple dumpling bubbling in a pot, tatties in their jackets in another, a great panful of turnips, and stew with a rich gravy 'hottering' at the side.

Mother had baked a sponge cake and some toddie scones in honour of Sonny's visit. They were cooling on the table beside me. And now, following the churning, we would have pounds of freshly-made butter to take home with us.

We had not come just for the food. The object of our visit was to rake through the garret to find objects for the Jumble Stall at the forthcoming Bazaar. Though I had not been deemed good enough to open it, I had been made convenor of the whole jing-bang, and had elected to run the Jumble Stall myself, feeling I would be more at home with junk than with Fancy Goods, Flowers, or Home Baking.

Mrs Sturrock could look after that lot.

It had been announced from the pulpit that contributions would be received at the Manse. So the morning room (sometimes known as the empty room) was already cluttered with cracked vases, fire irons, pokers, pictures, broken chairs, an old gramophone, a rocking horse, several jelly pans, mirrors and derelict teapots. There were even some discarded spectacles, a set of false teeth, and a mixty-maxty lot of what Oor Net called 'joolry'. Old pendants with stones missing, beads, bangles, and brooches.

'Jings Geordie! What's this?' she said, rummaging amongst the rubbish.

'Don't know! It looks like a marble. No! I believe it's a glass eye.'

So there was variety, if nothing else.

I had taken my duties seriously enough to tap the gentry for contributions, but I was disconcerted when I called at the Colonel's and he himself came to the door.

'Halt!' he shouted, though I had come to a standstill on the doorstep. 'Who goes there?'

'It – it's just me, sir.'

'What's your object?' he rapped out.

'Well – er – I'm looking for junk for the Bazaar.'

'Stand at ease.'

I waited for ages and thought he must have forgotten all about me, but suddenly he came back carrying a hunting horn, an old topee, and a pair of military-looking leggings, which he thrust at me and disappeared back into the house.

I was at a loss whether to accept them or not, but luckily I met his lady-wife as I made my way down the drive. When I consulted her she said, 'Good riddance! But, I warn you, he'll probably buy them back at the Bazaar.'

As it happened he did. First he pounced on the topee and tried it on for size, then the leggings which he found fitted him perfectly. Finally he picked up the hunting horn. 'I say! Haven't seen one of these for years. Must buy it. How much, fellow?'

'Sixpence for the lot, sir!' So he went off as happy as a sandboy delighted with his bargains.

It was surprising what the gentry considered junk. Lady Victoria was all for giving me a tiara which, though tarnished, was far too valuable – in my opinion – to be discarded. Besides, I did not foresee a ready sale for such an impractical item. Unless Mrs Stout fancied it for one of her concert appearances. So the Lady exchanged it for an old trinket box which could be converted into a sewing basket.

At the last moment I rescued a ring lurking in a corner.

'Oh! I think that's my engagement ring,' said her ladyship vaguely. 'Perhaps I'd better keep it.'

Aileen provided some books, much too 'heavy' for Annie S. Swan fans. *Decline and Fall of the Roman Empire*, *Foxe's Book of Martyrs*, and others of that ilk. I fell on some myself and put what I considered to be a fair price into the kitty, a tin biscuit box which I was keeping for that purpose.

Miss Calder, whose house was bungful of junk, refused to part with any of it. 'Never mind!' I said, not wanting to coax her, and went away back to the Manse. But presently she appeared at the door, carrying an old lamp and telling me how reluctant she was to part with it. She went on and on till I felt like handing it back and shouting, 'Oh! Just keep the thing!'

'You'll be sure to price it properly,' she insisted. 'It's much too good to be given away as a bargain.'

In the event, it was one of the few things on my stall that didn't sell, so Miss Calder got her treasure back!

One way and another I had gathered enough goods to overflow the stall, yet here we were, the minister and I, about to raid the farmhouse garret. It was really only an excuse for another trip home. Besides, I had my eye on the old fiddle for Wee Wullie.

But first I wanted to savour the pleasure of being free, if only for a few hours.

I went outside to gulp a breath of my native air. It was taking me longer this time to wind down. Surely I wasn't becoming too perjink!

'Nane o' your airs an' graces wi' me, ma lassie,' Jessie had admonished me when I was recounting some tale about my activities in the Village. I had not been boasting, just telling her; but she soon knocked me flat. Could she be a little jealous, thinking I was getting away from her? But I wasn't. It was her precepts I still followed, whatever I did.

I thought she was a little slower, a little bent; she who had always been so straight-backed.

'Och! There's nobody in the Village a patch on you, Jessie,' I assured her.

But it took a little wheedling. 'To tell you the truth,' Mother had whispered to me, 'I think she misses you.' And didn't I miss her?

I tried to fetch and carry for her, to lift the heavy churn and to help her with the milk pail, but that only made her cross. So I took her advice to get 'oot ma road' and ran like the wind to the big tree, aiming to climb it. But the swing was there, so I sat in that for a while and shoogled backwards and forwards. I called to Tam and Wull as they came clopping past with their Clydesdales and to Jock-the-herd who stopped to have a word with me. Just one word at first.

'Uh-huh!'

I uh-huhed him back while he leant on his crook and took a close look at me.

'Man-lassie! Ye're nae different.'

Thank goodness for that!

But, of course, I *was* different.

Hardly a woman of the world, but gaining a little more self-reliance. Learning, alas! to dissemble, sometimes saving an awkward situation by telling half-truths instead of sticking to Jessie's black or white, right or wrong. ('No! I don't think the minister's in. Could you leave a message?') I didn't know if God would forgive me, but I knew Jessie wouldn't.

But och! I hadn't altered all that much.

'Give me a swing, Jock! Go on! Higher! I want to see right over the treetop.'

It was like old times with Jock grunting as he heaved me higher and higher, faster and faster. I forgot all about Mrs Sturrock, the Women's Guild, and the Schemes of the Church. Swing high, sweet chariot! I could see over the treetop, as far as the ruined castle on the hill, as far as the Cheviots, almost as far as heaven. It was great.

'Man-lassie! Ye'll need to come doon. I'm fair sweetin',' groaned Jock, calling for a barley.

Someone else was calling. Jessie from the kitchen door, waving her apron and shouting that the meal was on the table.

After that the garret.

It was strange mounting the creaky stairs of my old gaol, knowing the door would not be locked behind me, that I was not being sent to solitary confinement, but could cut my sentence as short as I pleased. The musty smell brought back many memories. It had been a happy prison for me, except when they forgot to let me out and I was left in the lonely darkness.

I could rummage in the treasure chest – the old kist – and dress up the dummy in feather boas and finery. I could sit in the rickety rocking chair and read to my heart's content. The battered books were still there, spilling over in untidy heaps on the floor. *Woman at Home, The Quiver, Spurgeon's Sermons.* The dressmaker's dummy was still there, too, leaning against the wall with a torn sheet covering her nakedness.

And there in a corner lay the old fiddle.

'There it is!' cried H.J., coming up behind me and pouncing on the old violin. 'I had a feeling it was up here.' He examined it this way and that. 'I was thinking of getting it restrung and giving it to Wee Wullie.'

I didn't say a thing beyond, 'What a good idea!' But my heart warmed to H.J. for thinking of it; and after all Wee Wullie would appreciate it more, coming from God.

We collected a few items: bellows, a biscuit barrel, the wooden cradle which had been my first resting place, and an old clotheshorse which Jessie called a winter-dyke. We packed them all into the Baby Austin, and before we left Mother called me aside.

'What's up?' I asked in alarm.

'We've decided to buy you a frock. An evening dress.'

'What for?'

'The Ball.'

'Oh that!' It was to be a county ball. Some of the gentry

had invited H.J. and he was keen to go. Sonny had to take me as a partner, so I had better not look a sight.

'Can I choose it myself?' I asked. Otherwise it would be blue or green. I wanted red.

'No!' said Mother firmly, and a date was set when we would meet in Berwick to make the purchase. Oh well! It would be better than nothing. And anyway I had used up all the curtain material.

Jessie wanted to give me a parting present, a ginger kitten, one of Blackie's brood. I wanted to take her but H.J. put his foot down. 'We've got enough palaver with that puppy. You know what would happen! The Manse would be overrun with cats in no time.'

So I had to hand the kitten back to Jessie.

'You're not going to drown her?' I asked anxiously.

'Daursay no! I'll keep it masel'.'

'What'll you call her, Jessie?'

'Ginger,' said Jessie. 'Efter you!'

I tried to give her a hug but she fended me off. 'I'll give you a ring soon, Jessie,' I promised.

'Please yoursel',' she grumped; but she waved the kitten's paw to me as we drove off.

Back to the Manse. Change gear and throw off childish things. Back to countless meetings anent the Bazaar. They were held in the drawing room and invariably ended in squabbles which I could not control. It amazed me to see such jealousy between the stall holders. I felt like knocking their heads together.

'What does it matter?' I tried to intervene.

But it mattered to them whether their stall was at the top of the hall or the bottom. I changed my position several times to fall in with their plans.

'Put me anywhere. I'm only junk.'

But no! I was the Lady of the Manse and had to be seen, junk or no.

Sometimes the wrangling got so heated I was tempted to thump out 'Pop Goes the Weasel' on the piano. Instead, I rang the jangling bell as a signal for Oor Net to trudge upstairs with the tea. She trundled in a trolley and a truce was called while the ladies helped themselves to scones, cakes and biscuits from the three-tiered stand.

If the minister joined us all was sweetness and light. No quarrelling in his presence. 'Oh yes! We're getting on splendidly. It's all going smoothly. Can I pass you a scone?'

He didn't talk about the Bazaar but stood on the hearthrug nibbling his scone and regaling them with tales about everything under the sun. His harem listened attentively while he related his encounter with an eccentric character who had buttonholed him in the Village street, about his proposal to hold a sports day for the young folk, of what happened one Sunday when Leckie the beadle, saw a mouse in the vestry. A kirk moose!

'My! He's awful human, the minister,' the ladies told me, smiling benignly, when he left to go back to the study. But the smiles did not last long.

The squabbling started up again. Who was to be in the platform party at the Opening? The minister, of course. He would be introducing Annie S. Swan. And: '*She*'ll have to be there.' (This was me.) Mrs Sturrock? Or Miss Wotherspoon, the treasurer? And what about the gentry? Was Lady Victoria coming?

I switched off, and willed myself back to the swing under the big tree at home. How fresh the air felt on my face! Higher, Jock, higher! I could see the peaks of the Eildon hills cleft in twain . . .

'Well, that's settled,' said Mrs Sturrock, rising to her feet. 'You'll present the bouquet.'

'What bouquet?'

'For Annie Swan, of course! Just after she's declared the Bazaar open. I wonder what her favourite flowers are?'

They began to catter-batter again on their way downstairs, about the different merits of roses, sweet peas, carnations, gladioli.

I made my only sensible suggestion of the afternoon.

'Why not consult the Major's wife? She has a garden full of flowers and could make you a nice mixed bouquet.'

'That's not a bad idea,' conceded Mrs Sturrock; and the others looked at me with a little respect as I ushered them out of the door.

'Michty God!' said Nettie, collecting the teacups. 'It's gettin' close. I wonder if Annie S. Swan's as excited as us?'

'Not her!' I said to myself. 'She'll be in the middle of a chapter and won't be giving us a second thought.'

I could hear a ping-ping-pinging from the study. The minister was putting new strings on the old fiddle. I hadn't said a word to Wee Wullie about it. Leave that to God.

But though he was not interfering with the ladies and their committees, H.J. was not being inactive about the Bazaar. Why not get the male members of the congregation involved, too?

'But a bazaar's just for women,' protested the elders.

Not at all, said the energetic minister, and proceeded to convene a men's committee. They could have all sorts of moneyspinners as sidelines in the small hall. Or outside if the weather was fine. Clock golf, for example, a coconut shy, hoop-la, a treasure hunt for the children. Raffles? No! Mr Sturrock turned his face and his thumbs down at that. There must be no hint of gambling in the kirk. Well then, said the minister, what about an Aunt Sally?

134

'And you can be in charge of it, Mr Sturrock!'

I had been donated a body, a dummy like the one we had in the garret at home. When she was toshed up she bore a striking resemblance to old Miss Calder. She would be the very thing for Aunt Sally.

I made the men pay for the purchase. (Another two shillings in the biscuit tin.) They grew quite enthusiastic over the project and I admired H.J.'s skill – or was it finesse? – in getting them all involved.

On the day itself there was a great hustle and hammering as the men got down to the business of erecting stalls, trestle tables, setting up the coconut shy and laying out the clock golf. They even offered to cart the junk down to my stall; and I had to take care that the hall table did not go with it as well. The jokey elder was all for taking Oor Net. 'She'd mebbe mak' a hauf-croon.'

'Awa' ye go!' said Nettie, shaking a duster at him. 'I'm worth five bob ony day!'

We had invited the Opener for lunch, but she refused. She was coming straight from Edinburgh in a car, but thank you for thinking of it, she wrote. I was the one who was thankful not to have the added strain of providing a special lunch for the guest of honour. As it was, I was running like a harrier at the last moment, and was lucky to arrive at the hall, fully dressed, gloves and all, in advance of Herself.

Mrs Stout, who was helping at my stall, had put on her best hat with a bird of prey perched on top; and Mrs Sturrock was wearing her fur coat, though it was a scorching day as her purple face indicated. I had nothing better to wear than my good costume and green hat, but I pinned a bunch of violets in my lapel and hoped for the best.

The minister waited outside for the car to arrive and we heard a cheer as Annie S. Swan came sailing in. She was a pleasant plump lady, like a pouter pigeon, deep-chested, serene, sure of herself. I sat on the platform beside her while the minister made his opening remarks. I had primed him beforehand about her writings and reputation, and fortunately he made his speech short, realizing nobody wanted to listen to him while she was there.

When she rose to speak she bowed serenely, accepting the applause as her due. I watched everyone craning their necks and standing on tiptoe, Oor Net with her mouth wide open and her mother hushing Henry John in her arms, almost fainting with excitement.

Annie Swan had them all in the palm of her hand. It was a homely speech – more of a homily – but anything that fell from Her lips was a pearl. Even the men at the back of the hall stood as still as stookies, drinking in every word. She was the well-loved writer of their favourite stories, truly the people's friend, and they applauded her loud and long when she finally declared the Bazaar open.

I clapped as enthusiastically as the rest till I got a dunt from behind and someone handed me the bouquet to present. The Major's wife had done us proud with a magnificent bunch of multi-coloured flowers, tastefully arranged and tied with red velvet ribbon. Ought I to curtsey? I made a little bob and a little bow. 'Thank you, my dear,' she said graciously, and it was over.

The minister led her away to conduct her round the stalls. She was swamped with admirers touching the hem of her garments and begging for autographs. I made sure she met Oor Net and her mother, then I scuttled back to my stall.

Mrs Stout's bird of prey was wobbling excitedly as she sold baking tins, hammers, chamber pots, stone hot-water bottles, cracked teapots and cast-off clothing .

'How much?' an old wife was asking, holding up a pair

of long johns that had seen better days.

'Tuppence!' I said, making a quick assessment of the state of the garment and of the contents of her slender purse.

Though the others had meticulously priced everything on their stalls, we had decided to value only some of the better items and leave the 'rubbish' to be given away as bargains. Even so, the biscuit tin was filling rapidly, and Mrs Stout fingering the coins declared, 'We're doing awfly well. I wouldn't be surprised if we beat Fancy Goods. One in the eye for Mrs Sturrock!'

Though all the money would be lumped together into a grand total in aid of the Schemes of the Church, Miss Wotherspoon, the treasurer, would let each stallholder know how much she had made. So there was bitter rivalry to come out on top.

I didn't much care as long as we got rid of the goods, and I was relieved to see even the clothes pegs disappearing so rapidly.

The Pisky Parson had come to support the cause. ('Decent of him,' remarked H.J. 'I must remember to go to his Sale of Work when he has one. He's not a bad chap!')

'What can I sell you, Mr Montrose?' I asked, finding him looking in his vague way at the wooden cradle. I had no idea what his home circumstances were or if he had a family to fill the cradle. 'This used to be mine long long ago.' A lifetime ago.

'Well, in that case, it's got great value,' said the Pisky Parson, fishing in his pocket and bringing out a crumpled note. A ten-shilling note! 'Perhaps I could fill it with flowerpots.'

Babies would be better, I thought; but I accepted the note gratefully and added it to the contents of the kitty.

When the celebrity finally reached our stall on her

rounds there was little left but a mousetrap. 'The very thing I'm looking for!' she said, pouncing on it as if it was treasure-trove. 'I know it seems cruel, but I can't stand mice and my old tabby's grown too lazy to catch them. How much, my dear?'

I wanted her to accept it with our compliments, but she insisted on paying sixpence for it. We put it in a baker's bag for her, and she shook hands warmly with Mrs Stout before wandering off to the tearoom.

I had to go with her, for a special table had been set for the 'high heid anes', with the minister presiding and Mrs Sturrock pouring out. The best scones, pancakes, short-bread, homemade sponge cake and chocolate biscuits had been reserved for her benefit. While she ate a hearty tea I told her how much I had enjoyed her story about Alison and the doctor.

'Yes,' she agreed with no false modesty; 'I think it's one of my best. God has given me a great gift, my dear. It just pours out.'

I never let dab, of course, that I was attempting to write myself. She was the Queen Bee, and she waved like royalty when we surged to the door to see her off in her car. She had been a great success, we all agreed, and her stories would be read even more avidly by her admirers now that they had seen her in the flesh.

Well done, Annie!

When I got back to the hall I found Mrs Stout in her stocking soles and Miss Wotherspoon slipping her feet into an old pair of slippers. 'That's the worst of bazaars,' she moaned. 'Feet! My bunion's killing me. Still! It's in a good cause, and I think we've made a pickle siller.' A pickle was a quantity, and judging by her smug looks she was pleased with the amount.

The pickle, as announced proudly from the pulpit on Sunday, turned out to be nearly two hundred pounds, a record amount for a Village bazaar. Largely due to Annie S.Swan being such a good draw, and to the minister rounding up the men and the young folk who brought in a goodly sum with their extra activities.

Aunt Sally had been battered out of recognition, the clock golf had proved a great attraction, and even the lugubrious elder declared it was the first time he had enjoyed a bazaar. He almost smiled when he helped Miss Wotherspoon to count the takings.

But that was not the end of it. Mrs Sturrock decreed there would be a winding-up gathering in her house. A greetin' meetin', as such affairs were called, where everyone could air their grievances and suggest improvements for the next bazaar. The next? Help!

The ladies left no stone unturned as they partook of the tea provided, a far daintier one than they would have had in the Manse. Fancier even than Mistress Niven's. Mrs Sturrock had laid on all the niceties. Wee hand-embroidered napkins. Neat little sandwiches with the crusts cut off. Dropscones all the same neat size and shape. A rich cake with edible roses and violets decorating the top. Her grandmother's – or was it great-grandmother's? – fragile cups and saucers. Even a tea strainer, and a choice of Indian or China.

At first the talk was on a high level to match the food set before us, but gradually the tongues grew sharper and reputations crumbled with the cake. Miss Somebody's hat. What a sight! It was only fit for the Jumble Stall. And what about Mrs Somebody-Else? Always trying to mooch bargains. Set her up! And the Pisky Parson buying a cradle. Fancy that! As for Mrs Leckie pushing herself forward to speak to Annie Swan! And what about old Mr Thing turning up in his working clothes? He might at least have *shaved*.

Luckily the dividing out of the stall money had been

more or less equal, with Mrs Sturrock winning by a short head, so there were fewer recriminations on that score. And all agreed unanimously that Annie S. Swan had been 'fair marvellous'.

I wrote a warm letter of thanks to her, voicing our appreciation and hoping the mousetrap had come in handy.

'Yes, my dear,' she wrote back, 'I haven't seen a mouse since. I think it must have frightened them all away.' She went on: 'That was a very well-written letter of yours. Have you never thought of writing stories? You never know what you can do till you try.'

Oh! I'm trying all right, Annie! Just give me time.

Oor Net summed it all up by saying, 'See ma hand! *She* shook it. I'll never wesh it again!'

O dear! So how would we ever get the dishes done?

12. Revelry

It had never occurred to me that my brother was an eligible young man. Who in their sober senses would want to marry a minister and become Lady of the Manse?

Yet it appeared he was considered a good catch in the district. It was something old Sarah Googly said that opened my eyes.

I had gone into the shop to make a genuine purchase, some cough sweets for a tickle in the minister's throat, and had stopped for a short gossip with the old woman. I wanted to know how she had fared with His Reverence when he called to see her.

I had already asked him, 'Did you go and see old Sarah Googly?'

He nodded.

'What did you tell her?'

'About what?'

'Where she was going after she died.'

'Oh, that!'

He was tying his shoelaces at the time and did not look up. It always seemed to be a terrible task to H.J., as if he had never learnt properly as a child. He tried it in several ways. Left over right, turn under. Was it a sheepshank or a granny? No matter how he did it, his laces always worked loose; and after the effort of tying them he had lost the thread of the conversation.

So I asked old Sarah herself.

'Ay,' said she, 'he kens a' the answers, the meenister.'

What were the answers, I wanted to know, but old Sarah either couldn't or wouldn't tell me. So I was left in the dark, and it remained a mystery between her and the meenister.

I was taking my elbows off the counter preparatory to leaving when someone passing by the window caught sight of me. She stopped to wave and smile. I waved back. And that was that, as far as I was concerned.

But old Sarah had something to say.

'Watch her!' she muttered.

'What for?'

'Och! You're awful green,' said Sarah, shaking her head. Which was true enough. 'She'd like to get her hooks into the meenister.'

'Mercy me!'

The schoolmaster's daughter was a big gawky creature with buckteeth, older I think than the minister, very friendly and good-natured, but a bit of a nuisance with her constant calls at the Manse. She lived just across the road in the schoolhouse and often nipped over on some neighbourly errand.

I had to cope with her when H.J. scuttled out of sight if he saw her coming to the door. 'Her again!' he would groan.

'Is your brother in?' she would ask eagerly.

'I – er – I think he's just gone out.'

'Oh! I brought him some plums. I know he likes them. Will you tell him I was asking for him?'

'Oh yes, I will! Thank you.'

'I'll be back again soon.' A flash of teeth and she was gone.

But I never thought anything of it until now.

'Ay, an' there's mair than her!' said old Sarah darkly, but she did not specify who they were.

Good luck to them, I thought, as I walked up the Village street? Who could they be, I wondered? H.J. himself had shown no signs of being broody, but would I have noticed?

I did not realize I was walking in the middle of the street till the ringing of a bicycle bell interrupted my reverie. The District Nurse stopped to have a word with me, half off her bicycle, keeping one foot on the ground and the other ready to kick round the pedal.

'How's the minister?' she asked.

I took a closer look at her. *She* was surely not a contestant. Middle-aged, wholesome, fresh-faced, smelling of lysol and carbolic. Miss Paterson was a no-nonsense person. I liked her. She would have made a much better job at running the Manse than I did; but almost anybody would. However, I was sure she had no such thoughts in her head.

'The minister's fine,' I told her. 'Well, he has a bit of a cough.'

Miss Paterson looked interested. Professionally or was it personally?

'D'you want me to call in and have a look at him?'

'Och no! Don't bother. It's just a tickle. I've got some cough lozenges for him.'

We chatted for a while, then she kicked the pedal

round. 'Must be off! Perhaps I'll pop in and see your brother later.'

H.J. was playing the fiddle when I got back.

'How's your cough?'

He exaggerated it a bit for my benefit and I gave him the lozenges to suck.

'Miss Paterson'll maybe call in to see you,' I told him. I took note that he showed no special interest, so *she* was out! 'Would you like to cancel any of your meetings?'

'No, certainly not!'

He swallowed a lozenge and his cough at the same time. H.J. was not one to give anything up.

Certainly not the County Ball which was looming near.

He seemed particularly anxious to go, not I think for any romantic reasons, but to support the Major who was organizing it and who was calling him 'my boy' by now.

'You'll support me, my boy, won't you?'

'Certainly, Major.'

Sir Joseph and Lady Victoria were also to be in the party but Aileen, to my sorrow, could not go. It would be too strenuous for her, but she urged me to take note of all that happened and give her a full commentary on the evening's events.

'Maybe you'll get a story out of it,' she suggested.

But first I had to find myself a suitable dress. Mother fulfilled her promise to meet me in Berwick to make the choice. Her choice! She was in one of her haughty moods.

'Haven't you got a better petticoat than that!' she whispered, eyeing my skimpy undergarment when we were in the changing room of the smartest shop in Berwick.

'No, I haven't!'

Where did she imagine I got the money to buy

petticoats, or anything else? I had made it out of the last of the leftover curtain material and it did well enough for me. I felt my birse rising.

Calm down, I told myself! You're lucky to be getting a new evening dress. But it would have been nicer if I could have chosen it myself.

I did try. 'Could I not see some other colours?' I pleaded, knowing fine what the answer would be.

'No, you couldn't! This one, please.'

Mother smiled sweetly to the assistant, not to me. 'I think this will suit her best.'

It was blue, of course, a kind of cornflower colour. A floaty frock with a flounce at the bottom. It was all right, but not my choice.

'You don't look too bad,' conceded Mother, looking at me in the mirror. 'If only you could do something about your hair.'

'I'll try,' I promised, but not with much conviction.

Oor Net was all for crimping it with hot tongs but I managed to dissuade her. She was in a lather of excitement as she acted as my lady's-maid while I dressed. Lady Victoria had offered to lend me a tiara but I thought that was going a bit far. I accepted a wreath of roses from her, though in the end I didn't wear them. I just brushed and combed my locks into some kind of submission and hoped I would look 'decent'.

His Reverence was the one who took Oor Net's fancy when she saw him trigged out in his evening suit.

'Holy Moses!' she exclaimed. 'He looks mair like a gentleman than a meenister.'

There was nothing missing. Starched shirt front, cufflinks, white scarf, patent leather shoes, gloves.

Gloves! Little did H.J. know the trials and tribulations I had undergone over *them*! I had washed his white evening gloves in advance of the great event and left them hanging on the winter-dyke in the kitchen while I dashed out to do some shopping. When I came back Bush was sitting on the rug contentedly chewing. No need to ask what.

Luckily this happened before I went to Berwick on the frock-buying expedition; so when my elders and betters were taking tea afterwards in the Green Café, I slipped out on a lame excuse, and surreptitiously purchased a new pair of gloves. Bang went the small sum I had received recently from an Edinburgh newspaper; but at least the situation was saved and H.J. never noticed the difference.

(I have to record that by the end of the evening he had lost the gloves, so both they and my money were gone for ever!)

I felt sorry for Oor Net as I put on my silver slippers – they were new, too – and wished I wasn't leaving her behind, like Cinderella. But she was too occupied with Prince Charming to bother about me.

'Will I gie the meenister's back a dicht?' she offered, grabbing hold of a clothesbrush.

I could see she was getting a great kick out of the occasion and was needing no pity.

H.J. was a fusser about time, so we arrived far too early at the Major's residence where we were to join him and his wife in their great car and be chauffeur-driven to the ball. The Major, dressed in his regimentals, was whiling away the time playing the pianola, waiting for his wife to put the final touches to her finery. I sat beside him on the long stool while the 'Blue Danube' rolled round and round.

Later, when I had to dance with him, I had great difficulty keeping out of the way of his sword. I was used to partners like Jock-the-herd who wore tackety-boots at the country hops at home, but dancing with a sword was trickier.

'Would you like an ice?' asked the Major, mopping his brow.

'Oh yes, please!'

We left the ballroom and went to an inner room where folk were sitting out – the sit-ootery – and sat down at a little table. There were pink ices and white ices to be supped with dainty spoons, but we were only halfway through when his wife bore down on us.

'Come along! It's the Lancers.'

The Major groaned, hitched up his sword, and meekly followed her.

I had to keek at my wee card to see who was to be my partner. We had been given the cards as we came in; blue for the men, pink for the ladies, with little dangling pencils attached. Not knowing the names of some of my partners, I had scrawled 'tall with moustache' or 'fat with bald head', sometimes just 'Mr X'. I wondered what they had scribbled on their cards. 'Blue dress with tousled hair.'

Sometimes I danced with H.J. if he could not find a better partner. I have to say that my brother was a rotten dancer. In spite of being so musical, he seemed to have no sense of rhythm, and just bounced me around the room. I had to do little running steps to catch up with him. He was energetic, if nothing else.

Sir Joseph walked me majestically round the room, and turned me at the corners, doing what he considered to be a foxtrot, bowing now and again to the dowagers sitting on wee gilt chairs watching us.

It was only when I was claimed by a fresh-faced schoolboy, someone's nephew home from Eton, that I began to enjoy myself. We giggled like children as we romped round the room, and for a while I threw dignity to the wind till I noticed the dowagers frowning at us.

Quickly I steadied down, waltzed sedately with 'fat

with bald head', and at the end stood to attention while the band, half hidden by a shrubbery of foliage, played the National Anthem. After which we all joined hands and sang 'Auld Lang Syne', followed by three cheers for the Major who stood in the centre of the circle looking embarrassed.

Before we left we were given cups of hot soup. Oh! It did taste good. Then home in the wee sma' hoors, back to reality.

'Were you the belle o' the ball?' Oor Net asked eagerly in the morning.

'Of course!' I lied.

There was a photograph in the Berwickshire paper next week. I was half hidden by the Major's wife and looked no better and no worse than the rest, so that was all right.

Later that day Wee Wullie came rushing into the kitchen and turned a somersault at my feet.

'Ye'll never guess! No, never!' he said when he was in an upright position.

'What, Wullie, what?'

I had guessed all right but I wanted him to tell me.

'I've got a fiddle!'

'Never!'

'I have so!' His eyes were shining like stars. 'HE's got it for me. An' HE's gaun to gie me lessons. Isn't it great?'

He turned another somersault and I almost joined him on the kitchen floor. I was so pleased for his sake.

I suspected, all the same, that long months of misery lay ahead while Wee Wullie scraped away at his treasured fiddle. He kept it in the study and hung about, waiting patiently till God was free to give him a lesson. In between times he was allowed to steal in and practise on his own. It was agony listening to him.

The puppy used to yowl till I had to let him out of the back door. But Wee Wullie was persistent. One word of praise from his teacher sent him sky-high, and gradually we began to hear tunes emerging. His greatest moment was reached when he was allowed to play a simple duet with the minister.

'He's comin' on,' Oor Net said, cocking her ears to listen. 'That soonds like "Twinkle Twinkle Little Star". Jings Geordie! Fancy Wee Wullie bein' a mewsishun!'

Meantime we took another quick trip home so that Sonny could regale Mother with all that had happened at the great ball.

'How did *she* look?' Mother asked him.

'Oh! All right, I think,' said H.J., dismissing me.

So I went off on my own round to the byre where Jessie was milking the cows. I was pleased to learn there was a new servant-lassie in the kitchen to help her though she was a 'stupid sumph' according to Jessie. But I think the old woman was enjoying licking her into shape. Jessie needed someone to rage at; and Phemie, though empty in the head, had a strong pair of hands.

'She's got a lot to lairn, that article!' And who better to teach her than Jessie?

I sat on the wee stool with a row of cats beside me as I used to do in the old days.

'Tell me a story, Jessie.'

'Howts! Ye're ower auld for stories.'

'No, I'm not! Tell me about the wee moudiwart.'

She dug her head into the brown cow's side and I thought she had taken the strunts, but at last she gave in.

'A'weel, ance upon a time . . .'

I listened to the familiar words and then I wasn't listening. I was off into a dwam, hypnotized by the atmosphere: the hot breath of the cows, the miaowing of the cats sitting by their saucers, the rustle of the straw, the rhythm of the milk splashing into the pail, the sound of Jessie's voice. I was away back in my childhood and wished this moment could last for ever. But like the story it came to an abrupt end.

'That's it, lassie! Get oot ma road.'

She would not let me carry the milk pail into the house. 'Gang oot an' get a braith o' air. Ye need some colour in your cheeks. Ye're lookin' awfu' shilpit.'

(Shilpit meant peelly-wally, and peelly-wally meant . . . shilpit! Wan-faced and sickly-looking.)

I hied off to the hill where the wind whipped some red into my cheeks and blew away the cobwebs. I made straight for the ruined castle and climbed up the crumbling battlements where I could sit gazing across to the Carter Bar, hunching my shoulders against the strong wind.

I watched the far-off figures on the main road, recognizing the postie on his bike and the baker with his horse and cart. Many a time he had given me a lift to school, which always made me late for we had to stop at each cottage door delivering pan loaves and gingerbread. The school was scaling and I could see small groups of children making their way down the road, lashing out with their schoolbags and trying to trip each other up.

That shambling figure was surely Yorkie the tramp, and was that the Laird's car gliding by?

But never mind the people. I turned my eyes to the hills. They were what I missed most in Berwickshire. I swivelled my head towards the Eildons then back to the Cheviots. The hills of home. Keep this vision in your mind's eye, I told myself . . .

Too late I heard a warning shout and almost toppled from my perch.

There were two kinds of dangers on the hillside. The first was the bull who sometimes roamed loose and could rampage if he was in a nasty mood. The second was more terrifying.

''Fore!''

A golf ball whizzed past my ear missing me by a whisker. H.J. and Father, dressed in plus fours, had come up to the hill to play a round of golf and were slicing their shots in the strong wind.

Nowadays it was dangerous for me to linger at the castle since they had converted the hill into a rough-and-ready golf course with little flags set up at intervals to mark out the greens. They did not stay upright for long but were either knocked down by the bull or nibbled by the sheep.

It was an adventurous up-and-down course with each hole christened comically by Father. Crossing the Styx, Death Valley, the Himalayas, the Grand Canyon, Impossible! And as most of the battered golf balls disappeared down rabbit holes, he declared the hill would turn into a rubber plantation one day. They played with ancient clubs called niblicks and mashies, and displaced so many divots that Jock-the-herd complained, 'They're turnin' the hill upside-down. There'll be nae gress left for the sheep if they gang on like this. Daft eediots!'

But it was 'sport' and the pair of them would play till the last ball was lost; and even in the darkness the eediots were daft enough to continue, carrying a lantern to light their way.

The sheep who did not understand ''Fore!'' sometimes received direct hits. So did Jock, and on one occasion had a bump on his brow to prove it; but now as soon as he caught sight of a plus four he took avoiding action.

'Come doon!' he yelled to me, but I was half doon already. 'Ye're no' safe sittin' up there like a hoodie-craw. No' when that pair's on the loose. Fancy wastin' time chasin' after a wee ba'. They're gite!'

Gite meant daft, but there was nothing gite about Jock when he wanted to escape from danger. I had to run to catch up with him.

'How are you, Jock?' I asked breathlessly.

'I'm fine!' He climbed over the dyke into safer territory. Then he looked at me and said something that nearly bowled me over. 'Man-lassie! I hear ye're doin' no' bad doonbye.'

I could feel the colour rising to my face. 'No' bad' was the highest compliment Jock could give, like awarding the VC. But was it true? Was I really in my muddled way doing not badly? And who had told Jock?

I had forgotten about 'doonbye' in my delight at being back home again. Now I turned my thoughts towards the Manse and for the first time looked forward to returning there, almost as if it was home.

Yet when we drove off down the bumpy road and I had exchanged waves with the cottage wives, I turned as usual to take a last look at the shabby old farmhouse and I knew there was nowhere on earth to take its place.

That was my real home.

13. The Swarry

It was an ordinary day at the Manse, as peaceful as it ever was with the doorbell ringing, Bush barking, and Wee Wullie scraping away at his fiddle.

Henry John – the baby, not the minister – was lying on the bed in the servant's room, mewling and puking. Oor Net was supposed to be in charge of him while her mother was doing some shopping, but I could see out of the window that she was playing kick-the-can in the school playground.

Let the lassie enjoy herself! I was getting on fine rolling out pastry for the dozens of sausage rolls I was about to bake. The Pisky Parson raised his hat to me as he passed and I waved a floury hand to him. I wondered how he was getting on with the cradle? The baby began to cry and I tried to soothe him with one of Jessie's old ditties.

Ally-bally, bally-bally-bee.
Sittin' on your Mammy's knee,
Greetin' for anither bawbee
To buy Coulter's candy.

Henry John liked the sound so I had to continue humming. Was *he* going to be a 'mewsishun', too, like Wee Wullie? I hoped not. One was enough.

Ally-bally . . .

Suddenly I remembered.

Tonight was the great night of the Kirk Soiree, a social gathering where all the parishioners met in a friendly atmosphere and the minister mingled with his flock in a relaxed mood, more like an ordinary human being than a pastor.

The Swarry, it was called in the Village.

It was to be a much grander affair than the ones I had attended back home, where we were given our cookie buns in paper pokes which we blew up and burst with a bang after consuming the contents, where the entertainment consisted of the visiting ministers telling funny stories, Mary-Ann and the beadle singing 'The Crookit Bawbee' and the rest of us giggling as we exchanged sweetmeats called conversation lozenges.

May I kiss you darling? Not tonight!

We were to have conversation lozenges tonight at the Swarry, donated by old Sarah Googly, but we were not to be fed from paper pokes. It was to be a 'boofay' provided by the ladies of the congregation.

That was why I was baking so many sausage rolls. And that was why I had better hurry up for I had a hundred other things to do. The brethren were coming to support H.J. at the Swarry and would expect to be given a meal at the Manse beforehand. Some of them would be staying overnight. I had beds to make, shirts to iron, fires to light . . .

The doorbell rang.

'Shut up, you!' I said to Henry John and scuttled along the passage to answer the summons.

Aileen and her dog Jasper were on the doorstep. 'I'm not stopping,' she said hastily. 'I know you're busy. But I just had to tell you. I've had an acceptance!'

'Oh Aileen! Wonderful! Tell me!'

'It's only a little article. I took your advice and wrote about walking the dog. That Edinburgh paper has taken it.'

'Oh! Congratulations!'

We shook hands as if we had both won the Nobel Prize. Then I had reluctantly to leave her and attend to the bawling baby.

I rapped on the window to attract Oor Net's attention. The schoolmaster's daughter saw me and gave me one of her smiling waves. She was on her way across the road, but I mouthed, 'He's OUT,' so she turned on her tracks after another flash of teeth. Nettie gave a last kick to the can and came trailing back. Meantime the doorbell was jangling again.

'You took long enough to come,' grumbled Miss Calder, standing on the doorstep with her yapping pug at her heels.

'I'm busy . . .'

'You young folk, you never have time for anything!' snapped Miss Calder. 'I expect you're going to this awful Soiree tonight.'

'Well, yes! Are you coming, Miss Calder?'

She tossed her head. 'Wild horses wouldn't drag me!' Then to my surprise she thrust a large tin box into my hands. 'Toffee! I meant to make fudge but I boiled it too long and it turned out hard, but it'll be good enough for the Soiree.'

'Oh thank you, Miss Calder, it's very kind of you . . .'

'Rubbish! Mind! I want the box back.'

Nettie and I sampled the toffee as we hurried about our business. The lumps were all stuck together and it was difficult to separate them, but my heart warmed to Miss Calder for making the effort.

The next time the bell rang Oor Net went to answer it. She came back looking white about the gills.

'It's thon Colonel. He tell't me to stand at ease. I dinna ken what he wants.'

'I'll go and see,' I said, shifting my toffee to the corner of my mouth.

The Colonel was marking time on the doorstep. 'One-two! One-two!' He had a basket over his arm. 'Hullo, fellow!' He gave me a quick salute. 'Is His Holiness in?'

'No, sir,' I replied, then added with relief, 'but he's just coming in the gate.'

The Colonel abandoned me and turned to H.J. who took him by the arm and conducted him into the house. Wee Wullie rushed out of the study and I gave him a hot sausage roll to eat.

It was to be a momentous night for the young musician who was to make his debut at the Swarry and I was to play his accompaniment. It was the piece that sounded like 'Twinkle Twinkle Little Star'. We had rehearsed it over and over again in the drawing room with me thumping out the tune and Wee Wullie saying, 'Haud on! I'm awa' ahint!'

I was heartily sick of it by now but it meant a lot to him, especially as God was to accompany us, too, playing a kind of obligato in the background. It was terrible.

What would happen, I had asked Wee Wullie, if he got

an encore? 'Michty God!' he exclaimed, echoing his big sister. 'I'll just need to play the same thing again.' I hoped not.

Today he could scarcely swallow his sausage roll. 'D'ye no' think we could have another wee shot up in the drawing room?' he inquired anxiously.

'Sorry, Wullie. No time. Anyway, you're perfect!'

'I doot it,' he sighed with commendable modesty, and agreed to take the puppy out for a run.

Miss Calder's was not the only contribution to be brought to the door that day. The bell seemed to ring nonstop as parishioners called with offerings for the cookyshine. Instead of delivering them straight to the church hall, everyone liked an opportunity to call at the Manse, hoping they might be invited in for 'a wee cup of tea'.

Nettie and I kept bumping into each other as we met head-on in the passage, and not for the first time I wished I was a centipede. Even the Colonel had brought a contribution, but the basket which should have contained a currant loaf was full of weeds from his rockery. When H.J. pointed out his mistake, he marched off quite happily to retrieve the loaf. He would return, if he remembered, to continue his discussion with His Holiness who was looking a little limp by now.

So was I by the time I had tussled with the big bolsters in the spare bedroom. The time whizzed by and the brethren arrived far too soon, rubbing their hands in expansive moods, expecting to be fed and watered. They drank copious cups of tea and wolfed down so many sandwiches and sausage rolls that Oor Net exclaimed, 'Michty God! There'll no' be nane left for the Swarry.'

She was toshing herself up in front of the kitchen mirror and there was a strong smell of frizzled hair as she wielded the hot tongs on her locks. But she looked nice with her face flushed and wearing a new pink dress I had helped her to make. I told her she looked a treat.

'Och! I'll pass mustard,' she replied, taking a last keek in the mirror, but I could see she was pleased with herself.

The star of the Swarry was undoubtedly the minister himself. Determined to make the evening go with a swing, he acted as Master of Ceremonies, led the community singing, played the fiddle, danced 'The Grand Old Duke of York' with Mrs Stout, even helped to pour out the tea. It was easy to see how the parishioners had taken him to their hearts. How could I help feeling proud of him as I heard flattering comments on all sides? Not just the oft-repeated, 'Isn't he awful human?' but, '*He*'s a real Christian!'

Well done, Sonny!

The evening was more secular than sacred, though we did our best to praise the Lord while still sucking our conversation lozenges. The lugubrious elder surprised me by passing me one with the motto *Hullo, dear* printed on it. I had nothing better than *Perhaps* to pass back to him, but at least it was in the shape of a pink heart.

The hall was transformed with potted plants and greenery to hide the dingy corners, and the 'spread' was laid out on a long trestle table. All kinds of home baking from sausage rolls to shortbread, and mince pies to meringues. Leckie grumbled about the crumbs on the floor but I hoped there might be some left over for the kirk moose.

Everyone ate heartily except Wee Wullie who had lost his appetite. His ordeal was still to come. 'I wish I was deid!' he kept muttering. 'I think I'll jouk oot the door.' Instead, he bit his lip and stuck to his guns. Or his fiddle. He could not let God down.

When the rest of us were replete we sat down on benches round the room and waited to be entertained.

Everyone put solemn expressions on their faces when the brethren got up to address them, but soon we were all convulsed with laughter. Imagine such godly men telling funny stories! We laughed heartily even if we had heard them before. Oh! If only they would be as witty in the pulpit.

Mrs Stout, at bursting point in her tightest frock, had her big moment when she got up to sing, 'O, whustle an' I'll come tae ye, ma lad.' All the men whustled back at her, including the brethren, and she blew them delighted kisses at the end. It was a great performance.

Wee Wullie got *three* encores and everyone knew the tune fairly well before he was finished! I thumped out the accompaniment on the piano while H.J. played an unobtrusive obligato in the background. At the third repeat the young musician grew so confident that he put in an extra twiddly-bit, by mistake or design.

After he had taken his bow H.J. shook hands with him and patted him on the back. 'O God!' gasped Wee Wullie, not addressing the minister, but just from relief. 'I've did it!' Then he looked around hungrily. 'Is there onything to eat? I'm stervin'!'

Some of the more strait-laced elders shook their heads doubtfully when, in order to involve the young folk and make the Swarry go with a swing, H.J. suggested having a few dances. There was nothing unholy in 'Stripping the Willow' or doing 'The Grand Old Duke of York'; and surely no one would be sent to purgatory for dancing the polka or even a waltz.

Miss Steele, the organist, offered to oblige by playing the piano, and in the end even the elders got up and joined in, looking less stuffy as they swung their partners round the room.

After waltzing with one of them I sat down, breathless, beside Mrs Sturrock and took stock of everyone.

These could all be characters out of a storybook, I thought, looking around at the animated faces. Annie S. Swan could have written about them. Even *I* might. Then suddenly I realized they were real people, not strangers to me any more. They were my friends, almost like Jessie and Jock-the-herd. I was no longer amongst alien corn.

I looked reflectively at H.J. as he moved around chatting pleasantly with his parishioners. What of his future, I wondered? Anything could happen. Maybe he would become Moderator, the highest office in the Church of Scotland. I tried to picture him in knee britches with ruffles at his wrists, consorting with the mighty. But I had a clearer picture of him running the hundred yards at the local sports, breasting the tape as winner.

And what about romance? When would he marry a proper Lady of the Manse and set me free? He was making straight for Miss Wotherspoon inviting her to take the floor with him for a polka (pity her poor feet!) but *she* was old enough to be his Mammy. And did I want to be free? Free to write from morning till night, as Aileen did, instead of in dribs and drabs . . .

Och! Who could foresee the future? Let it take care of itself. It was the present that mattered, here and now at the Swarry with my new friends.

I exchanged smiles with the schoolmaster's daughter, hoping in vain to be 'lifted' for a dance by H.J., and with Oor Net prancing past with a clumsy laddie as partner. Keep it up, Nettie! Enjoy yourself while you can and forget tomorrow's dirty dishes.

I hummed the tune Miss Steele was playing. *Thumb-one-two-three!*

Then Mrs Sturrock knocked me down with a feather.

'It was the best thing that happened to the parish,' she remarked.

I watched the minister whirling round with Miss Wotherspoon in his clutch. He was off the stot as usual. *Thumb*-one-two-three!

'Yes,' I agreed, pleased as always to hear H.J. praised. 'The minister's doing a great job.'

'Oh!' said Mrs Sturrock, turning to look at me. 'I wasn't talking about him. I was meaning *you*.'

Holy Moses!

BESTSELLING SCOTTISH BOOKS
FROM ARROW

All these books are available from your bookshop or news-agent or you can order them direct. Just tick the titles you want and complete the form below.

☐	A BREATH OF BORDER AIR	Lavinia Derwent	£1.25
☐	GOD BLESS THE BORDERS	Lavinia Derwent	£1.25
☐	LADY OF THE MANSE	Lavinia Derwent	£1.75
☐	ONE SMALL FOOTPRINT	Molly Weir	£1.25
☐	ROCKS IN MY SCOTCH	Angus MacVicar	£1.25
☐	BEES IN MY BONNET	Angus MacVicar	£1.75
☐	SILVER IN MY SPORRAN	Angus MacVicar	£1.75
☐	BRUACH BLEND	Lillian Beckwith	£1.60
☐	BEAUTIFUL JUST	Lillian Beckwith	£1.60
☐	LIGHTLY POACHED	Lillian Beckwith	£1.60
☐	GREEN HAND	Lillian Beckwith	£1.60
☐	THE HILLS IS LONELY	Lillian Beckwith	£1.60
☐	A ROPE – IN CASE	Lillian Beckwith	£1.60
☐	THE SEA FOR BREAKFAST	Lillian Beckwith	£1.60
☐	A SHINE OF RAINBOWS	Lillian Beckwith	£1.75

Postage _____

Total _____

ARROW BOOKS, BOOKSERVICE BY POST, PO BOX 29, DOUGLAS, ISLE OF MAN, BRITISH ISLES

Please enclose a cheque or postal order made out to Arrow Books Limited for the amount due including 15p per book for postage and packing for orders both within the UK and overseas.

Please print clearly

NAME ....

ADDRESS ....

....

Whilst every effort is made to keep prices down and to keep popular books in print, Arrow Books cannot guarantee that prices will be the same as those advertised here or that the books will be available.